Ex Libris

Margaret E. Asovin

To Dear Margaret
with my very very best wishes
affectionately
Ellen (v. Ewen-Pugh)
Bishop's Castle
Aug. 1995

The Reluctant Phoenix

The Reluctant Phoenix

Ellen von Einem Pugh

The Pentland Press
Edinburgh – Cambridge – Durham

© Ellen von Einem Pugh, 1994

First published in 1994
by The Pentland Press Ltd
1 Hutton Close
South Church
Bishop Auckland
Durham

All rights reserved
Unauthorised duplication
contravenes existing laws.

ISBN 1-85821-203-1

Typeset by Carnegie Publishing Ltd, 18 Maynard St, Preston
Printed and bound by Antony Rowe Ltd, Chippenham

I wrote this book for my very special family: my children Marion and Tom, and my grandchildren Fiona, Raffaele, Ben and Sandy. Last, but not least, it is for my husband Leslie, without whose encouragement *The Reluctant Phoenix* would never have been written

Your pain is the breaking of the shell
  that encloses your understanding.

Even as the stone of the fruit must break,
  that its heart may stand in the sun,
    so must you know pain.

And could you keep your heart in wonder
  at the daily miracles of your life,
    your pain would not seem less wondrous
      than your joy;

And you would accept the seasons of your heart,
  even as you have always accepted the seasons
    that pass over your fields.

And you would watch with serenity through
  the winters of your grief.

Much of your pain is self-chosen.

It is the bitter potion by which the physician
  within you heals your sick self.

Therefore trust the physician, and drink his
  remedy in silence and tranquillity:

For his hand, though heavy and hard, is guided
  by the tender hand of the Unseen.

And the cup he brings, though it burn your lips,
  has been fashioned of the clay which the Potter
    has moistened with His own sacred tears.

KAHLIL GIBRAN
The Prophet

Acknowledgements

I would like to thank my friend Madeleine Fetherstonehough for her valuable initial help in getting this book on its way. I am particularly indebted to my dear friend and editor (in that order) Eve Wright Thompson, whose help in sorting out a maze of experiences, clarifying issues and tirelessly editing and typing the manuscript, was priceless. I am infinitely grateful to Leslie, my husband, who never complained about a late, or very late, lunch or supper, but who instead fired my confidence with his enthusiasm and continuous encouragement. Credit, too, must go to my dear daughter-in-law Hélène Pugh and her husband, my son-in-law Ashley Pugh. Their articulate, clever and wonderfully witty writings have always been a source of inspiration to me. Their sincere and honest judgment was more important than they will ever know.

ELLEN VON EINEM PUGH

Author's Foreword

THIS BOOK is an autobiography, endeavouring to gather the different threads of my rather dramatic life into a pattern which makes sense to me and which will, I hope, strike a chord with people who can identify with it. Not necessarily with the details, but rather with the essentials of the struggle that I experienced in finding my way through countless obstacles to the simple inner state of peace and joy which, I believe, is our true nature but against which we often kick and fight until, reluctantly, as in my case, we are drawn into the light.

The book is based on my life story, but the format I have chosen is not chronological. With the use of flashbacks and conversations, I have tried to move around the story in such a way as to illustrate the inner momentum of the forces which served to change and shape me.

The story is based loosely around a visit I made to New York City in 1987, where I unexpectedly met an old German friend whom I first knew in 1945 when the Russians were invading Poland and East Germany. During my stay in New York, events occurred which caused me to recall experiences in my life that were the catalysts for change and awareness. It was here in New York, between 1967 and 1973, that I was forced by dire circumstances to meet the challenge of life itself, stripping bare my illusions of self and the world and thereby emerging a more authentic person.

ELLEN VON EINEM PUGH

Foreword

In this foreword, I would like to draw from the wisdom of Gibran.

> . . . as love crowns you so shall he crucify you. Even as he is for your growth, so is he for your pruning.
> Even as he ascends to your height and caresses your tenderest branches that quiver in the sun.
> So shall he descend to your roots and shake them in their clinging to the earth.
> Like sheaves of corn he gathers you unto himself.
> He threshes you to make you naked.
> He sifts you to free you from your husks.
> He grinds you to whiteness.
> He kneads you until you are pliant;
> And then he assigns you to his sacred fire, that you may become sacred bread for God's sacred feast.
> All these things shall love do unto you that you may know the secrets of your heart, and in that knowledge become a fragment of Life's heart.

Ellen's life-story is such a rich tale of much pruning and threshing, all in the name of love. For what has emerged from the threshing floor of life is a very loving being, one whose greatest gift as a therapist is a sincerely caring attitude.

Life is about learning and sometimes the lessons are not easy to experience. But despite more than a few hard knocks in her life Ellen, far from turning from love in a wave of cynicism as many of us might do, has grown within the mantle of love. Now, in later life, she affirms the healing power of love in all her courses and lectures and urges those who seek her help to put themselves in touch with the universal power of love available to each one of us at any moment.

This book is another form of the gift Ellen offers to others for she hopes it will inspire and encourage those who struggle through love's pathways. We are all guides and signposts to each other on this journey that we share. I trust you will enjoy, as I have, the time spent in communication with this particular guide. Let her show you how you can come through the fire and laugh again, on your way to realising that you are but 'a fragment of Life's heart'.

EVE WRIGHT THOMPSON

Preface

It has required patience and persistent endeavour over the past two years to persuade my wife to overcome her reluctance to put pen to paper for a story I feel should be told. Reluctance is understandable, since this involves extracting sad memories from sealed sections of her mind, before they fade into oblivion.

Much has been written about the devastating consequences of the Second World War, of which the tyrant Adolf Hitler was the instigator, in league with his cohorts in their insane and mistaken vision of world domination. Less has been written about the inspired, far seeing, loyal members of the opposition to the Hitler regime, who so bravely contested the perpetrators of the holocaust, or of what took place behind the Maginot Line before these supposedly impenetrable obstacles were broken and freedom from fear, hardship and tyranny restored.

What were the experiences of those stragglers overcome by the brutal and ruthless advance of the Russian Army? My wife can tell first hand of the anxieties, deprivation, hardships and injuries she and her family suffered and her dismay at the destruction of timeless treasures, of magnificent cities on both sides destroyed in the cause of freedom and peace: Dresden, Coventry, Berlin, London, Munich, Manchester, and so on.

My wife's father was one time German Consul in New Zealand and he was, from that vantage point, enabled to gain a more balanced vision of the world. Eventually, back in Germany, he developed a world-wide business, exporting machinery and machine parts.

With the rise of Hitler to power, export ceased; he was faced with bankruptcy and was unable to recover large sums of money owed to him by clients abroad. However, he was instrumental in helping people to escape from Germany and was able to help them financially with those sums still due to him, until they became established.

He worked in co-operation with his close friend, Dr Karl Gördeler, Mayor of Leipzig at the time, the principal instigator in the plot to kill Hitler. With the help of Dr Gördeler, he was given a job in Poland to restore agricultural life in the devastated areas. His family found itself there when the Russian Army advanced from the east.

From there this true story will unfold, now that my wife has finally set to work with her pen!

H. L. Pugh, FRAS

Chapter 1

Macy's *fifth-floor snack-bar was teeming that Friday lunchtime as I surveyed the room, waiting my turn. I* walked over to the counter when a space suddenly became available and sat down. I was waiting for Joan, an old friend, who would join me in a few minutes.

As I sat waiting, I took in the familiar scene. Here in New York I had lived for over seven years some time previously. Those seven years, I now knew, had opened my eyes, my mind and my heart to many things – not least to a new view of myself and the world.

During that time I had experienced everything from cockroach infestation to gracious living. Those had been years of struggle, illness, turmoil and eventually a metamorphosis: years when it had been my fortune to come face to face with the widest possible range of people in some very close personal encounters; thrown into situations sometimes where I had to confront and come to terms with my own tumultuous past. In the process I had rediscovered my full capacity for loving life.

I had no desire to live here again. My European roots were stronger than those I had put down in the years in America, even though I would always be grateful for the things I had learned there. My sojourn in the USA had served a valuable purpose – that of bringing my European experiences into focus, at last.

'What can I get you, Ma'am?' the young waiter's voice brought me back with a bang. His eyebrows reached up into his crew-cut as he stood there, regarding me quizzically.

'I'd like a cup of coffee and a cheese and tomato sandwich,

please,' I said, giving the young man a big smile which he answered with a grin and a show of enormous white teeth.

'OK, sweetheart, coming right up.'

I recalled a day in this very snack bar (it was a cafeteria-style restaurant then) when I was startled by a fat and bossy Bronx woman who had elbowed her way through a group of people, waddled up to me and demanded, 'Whaddya use on your hair to make it go that colour?'

After a second's hesitation, I had replied politely. 'Oh, well, I use Rubinstein's Platinum Rinse on it, actually.' I smiled at the candid face that beamed at me.

'God, really? But how d'ya get those streaks in it?'

'Well, you see, it had started to get some white streaks in it quite naturally and the hair rinse turns the white streaks to platinum.'

'Well, whaddya know!'

And before I could say another word, the intruder had wheeled around and scuttled back to her place in the queue and was talking animatedly to her friend who stared at me.

The coffee came quickly and I was in need of another by the time the sandwich had arrived. 'Another coffee, please,' I said, causing several faces to look up and take notice of this strange lady who spoke English rather too well to be American or even English!

I became aware, too, at that instant, of another face looking at me and I realised that it had been doing so for some time. I turned my head very slightly to see a pert and very plump little woman, well on in years, with alert bright eyes which seemed to be looking right inside me.

We held our mutual gaze for a moment. I felt my heartbeat quicken and a deep emotion which I could not fathom come over me. It was as if something somewhere had been touched, a chord from long ago, and in a split second a wealth of emotions ranging from terror to great joy passed through me, and I found myself trembling with the strength of the experience.

Had the little lady then disappeared and never spoken, who knows how long it would have been before the complete memory would have surfaced.

'Is your name Ellen?'

The woman spoke with a distinct German accent, tinged with the flavour of Brooklyn. The sound of her voice and accent gave rise to more specific feelings, this time of a distant despair, and of a small garden and the scent of narcissus. Oh, where . . . ?

'Yes, it is,' I murmured, 'Who are you?' *My words came quickly, eager to reach the point of recognition, however many painful memories might be recalled.*

'Martha – do you remember ? – at Ranis.'

'Oh, Martha!' *I took a long, deep breath as memories of another time – another life? – came flooding back at last. I remained speechless for a minute, not quite able to accommodate this particular part of my past into the crowded and noisy milieu of downtown New York affluence and modernity and my present state of musing recollections of life here.*

At last I smiled and said with much feeling, 'It's great to see you, Martha. How on earth do you come to be here in New York? Do you live here now?'

Martha hesitated a moment. She did not reply immediately but instead rose to her feet and then came towards the counter where a seat had appeared next to me.

'This is wonderful, Ellen, fantastic! You know, I always hoped I'd see you again. Max and I, we were so lucky. After we all had to split up, we got a lift on a truck which went to Swabia. We stayed with a cousin up in the mountains until things got more organised and then Max wrote to his brother who had a grocery store in Brooklyn and he said come on over and we'll help you get started in the land of "opportunities". So here we are and we've been in New York ever since. Life has been really good to us here.'

She paused for breath and then continued, 'Only last week Max and I were talking about that time when you were praying in that tiny garden at the Steibers' house, and I heard you pleading with God to let your father see sense, and I was crying – so were you – do you remember, Ellen? Oh, how close we were then!'

I reached out a hand towards hers and together we shared a moment of quiet communication, of thoughts and love born of our shared experiences during the War so long ago now.

'Oh, yes, Martha! How could I forget? When I look back at that whole horrific train of events, I always think of you and those times in Ranis as a little haven in the midst of all that turmoil.'

'Ellen, what happened to you after? You look so well! I really feared that you might not survive after the way you were beaten up.'

I had to laugh. 'Thank you, Martha. I do feel much better now. If only you knew! Yes, that was the worst time I was beaten up, but not the last time, by any means. I've seen many changes and moved around a lot. But, as you can see, I'm still in one piece and I've learned a lot.'

We chatted some more and eventually, when my friend Joan arrived, we arranged to meet again and catch up.

That evening, at Joan's attractive brownstone house in Manhattan. I found myself recounting many of the memories that Martha's face had brought back to me so vividly – memories I realised that had lain buried deep within me for so long.

Long into the night Joan and I talked and her keen interest in those times brought up a wealth of pain and sorrow, mixed with powerful feelings of relief.

'You met Martha when you were fleeing from the Russian army?' she asked.

'Yes, she's inextricably connected with that part of my life.'

The New York evening was warm. We were surrounded by

In Joan and Stuart's garden, Manhattan, New York, 1985.

high trees in the delightful little garden which Joan and her husband Stuart had created in the heart of Manhattan. The distant hum of city traffic accompanied my reflections as I lost all sense of time in reliving those memories as she helped me unearth them.

Chapter 2

We had left my parents' house in Welun in the evening. My father had obtained a post in this small Polish town with the help of Dr Karl Gördeler, at the time Mayor of Leipzig and the leader of the unsuccessful bomb plot which had failed to kill Hitler. My father had been made responsible during this time for helping people in the vicinity to organise their agricultural needs.

I had returned to my family four months previously after having nearly been killed in a bombing raid at Mühlhausen. I had been acting in the local theatre there for the summer season while my little daughter Marion stayed with my parents. I was pregnant with my second child, and we had heard the previous day that the Russians were on the move westwards and might arrive any day. It was essential that we move quickly, so we took nothing but our suitcases filled with our most practical clothes, first aid items and a few small mementos. Our chauffeur took us in the car to the next town. Father and he were to make a return journey to collect our valuables from the safe – jewellery and other precious items which would, hopefully, make our journey and future existence easier, as we fled from the oncoming Russians who were rapidly advancing into Poland.

My mother, Marion and I were safely ensconced in a pleasant hotel near the railway station when my father set off with our chauffeur to return to Welun for our things. We knew we'd have a long wait and, after Marion went to sleep in the early evening, my mother and I began our long vigil.

At last, about two o'clock in the morning, we heard Father

returning. I had been dozing awhile and I awoke with a start. My father's face, gaunt and drawn, told his story before he even opened his mouth.

'Grete, Fiede, I'm afraid we are poor now. I couldn't get back – the Russians are there already.'

The full meaning of what he said sank into me. My mother flinched slightly and after a silent moment, she straightened her back. Her proud and lovely face was full of warmth and strength.

'No, we are not poor. We are alive and we have each other. This is far more than many people have. We are rich.'

There followed much talking. We talked of the past; we talked of the future. We needed to discuss our loss and its implications, and talk our way through to some sort of inner resolution before we could go forward on our journey.

By the end of that long night, we had promised each other that, no matter what, we would not talk of the material things we had had to leave behind at Welun. We would not express regret about having to relinquish the life style we had enjoyed. We would instead actively strive to focus our energies on the present, try to remain cheerful and think of encouraging and positive things to say, helping each other to overcome the difficulties that lay before us and to look forward to a brighter future.

My parents both had strong personalities, and my mother in particular was an advocate of mind over matter. I realise now what a significant moment this was for the three of us, and how crucial it was that we decided on this approach. Although it meant that the headache and grief for our 'loss' was pushed into the background and might need dealing with at some later time, it was a necessary postponement for those times – a life-saving tourniquet. For in the months that followed we saw literally thousands of refugees on the move, talked with many of them, heard their stories, empathised with their plights. And we observed several distinctly different ways that people had of dealing with their changed circumstances.

The following morning I awoke with a sense of excitement. It was a bright and frosty morning and I shivered, more with anticipation than with cold. We had had a long sleepless night and now we had to face a new life and a new world.

As we walked along the road away from the small hotel where we had spent the night, our breath froze in front of us, making little white clouds which rose in the still air. My father strode on ahead, my mother and I walking one on either side of little Marion. We each carried a suitcase containing all we now possessed.

The sun was beginning to melt the frost on the grass which grew along the road. After ten minutes walk, Breslau railway station appeared as we rounded a corner, and as we approached its grim walls, Marion's small gloved hands gripped ours more tightly and I murmured a few words of reassurance as she struggled bravely up the steep stone steps.

Once at the top I had to stop and rest; the exertion of carrying my heavy bag as well as the baby growing within me was too much for a moment. I remember looking up at the frozen windowpanes of the ticket office and noticing the beautiful patterns the frost had etched on them.

Slowly we made our way along the platform, skirting groups of weary-looking people, some of whom had obviously camped here all night. Their makeshift homes on the platform were made of suitcases, cardboard boxes, blankets, parcels tied with string – anything they could bring with them or find in the vicinity.

Families sat close together, small children wrapped inside greatcoats, mothers and grandmothers dispensing bread and biscuits. Elderly men, perhaps grandfathers, glanced anxiously down the track, following with their eyes the course of each new arrival along the platform.

As we made our own space to sit down, spreading out a rug and an extra sheepskin coat father had brought, I thought of my situation with a sudden poignant feeling of overwhelming sadness. I observed these family units, invariably without a father, huddled all around us and, studying their faces, I felt I was looking into their private lives, into their own intimate grief and sadness.

Three months earlier my husband had been reported missing, presumed dead. I wanted him here with me desperately. Grief welled up inside me as it struck me forcefully that the pain all around me united us all. Here I was, thirty years old, seven months pregnant, and mother of a lovely two-year-old girl, with much of my life ahead of me – or so I could presume. Yet without Klaus in my future, it was difficult to feel hopeful. No new goals had yet grown up to replace the old, now shattered, dreams. Indeed, the future was uncertain for all of us. We had this journey to face, the destination of which we were quite unsure. I stopped myself thinking of Klaus and what might have been. It was not the time to dwell on that. Now I was part of this family group, consisting of my parents, Marion, myself and my little stowaway; we had unknown and formidable times ahead.

How ironic! Here we were, fleeing from the Russians, in spite of the fact that my father had been deeply involved since before the War with the Resistance movement. He had helped scores of people to escape the repressive Hitler regime, by making his own impounded foreign funds accessible to them when they arrived in their new homelands in the West. Why were we now having to run for our lives from an Allied force? Why should we, who had felt so passionately for the plight of the Jewish people that we had dared to risk our freedom and endanger our own lives, now have to flee like criminals from the invading Russian army? Of course, there was no way the Russians could know our story. We looked German, we were German. There was no outward sign that showed we had worked against Hitler. We simply had to accept a sad state of affairs.

And yet, looking back, I realise that we were somehow fortunate. Something beyond ourselves seemed to enable us to cope with the myriad difficulties we faced over the following months. Nothing seemed to make sense. Events totally beyond our control swept us along. What had happened over the past twenty-four hours had been one of the most unfair twists of fate that I had yet experienced, but where is justice in times of war?

Many, like us, who had suddenly found themselves poor, threw themselves into the mainstream of events that were happening and tried not to look back. But others seemed to linger in a twilight world where they found it impossible to move forward from the 'good old times' they had left behind. They talked about wonderful homes and many splendid possessions, describing in infinite detail pieces of art and cherished objects, as if describing them would have the power to bring them back. Many tears flowed. Everyone has their own way of dealing with the inevitable, I thought. Maybe their hour of acceptance will come too. Some shell-shocked individuals were stuck in a nightmare world where they spoke little about their past, were unaware of the present and had no hope nor thought for the future. They lived their existence perfunctorily, the changes sweeping past them and engulfing them, eventually washing them ashore. If only we could hold on to our hopes and daily count our blessings.

The station was now quite crowded. Some people had camped out the previous night in the waiting room and were only just now emerging, as the sun rose higher and began to warm the cold day. They looked rough and grey, their tired faces telling the stories of their difficult journeys to this spot where we all waited for this exodus to continue, the outcome of which none of us could know. Rich and poor, young and old alike, waited calmly for the next train, if that existed . . .

Several hours later the sound of a train puffing and whistling far in the distance caused everyone to scramble to their feet and hastily break their makeshift camps. They forced items of clothing into already over-stuffed bags and gathered up children into their arms, the whole assemblage moving slowly towards the edge of the platform.

We looked at the sombre faces of the passengers as carriage after carriage went by, and we could see that the train was already quite full. Some of the anxious, grim faces were distinctly unwelcoming, others expressionless. There were youngsters riding on the ends of the carriages outside. How could there be space for us on board?

Luckily the train had to stop here for coal and water. I doubt if the driver would have stopped otherwise; his load was heavy enough already and there were no provisions left for anyone. A mad scramble ensued, as the waiting people endeavoured to find places on the train. Our little family group held back, our natural politeness making it feel wrong to push and shove, yet we were alert for an opening somewhere. Then I noticed that the occupants of the carriage beside us were gesticulating toward us, beckoning us to come aboard.

'Come on, bring that child, we'll make room for you,' an old gentleman said.

We didn't have to be told twice. One by one, we were raised bodily up and over the heads of the passengers by the attending Red Cross men and then lowered gently, gradually sinking down to find a place in the sea of bodies.

When it was my turn to be hoisted up, I looked out of the window and saw some little white bundles being carried from the train. A strong fascination gripped me, and I strained to see more clearly. In those few moments as I sank into the crowd, I realised with a sickening shudder what the thinly wrapped white shapes were: bodies of babies, frozen little forms, were being deposited onto the concrete platform.

The vision of these tiny frozen faces stayed with me during the long journey ahead. I made up a story to fit this sad scene, about an orphanage where food and fuel shortages had been so severe that many of the children died. But this story didn't answer the question – why had they been loaded onto this train and why were they being deposited there? My mind couldn't find an answer to the puzzle, and it continued to haunt me.

The other passengers seemed to be cheered by the presence of Marion and those who had seats were glad to take it in turns to have her sitting on their laps. How they got that door shut again after the introduction of still more people into the carriage, I'll never know, but after a bit of a struggle it swung to and we waited to depart. Eventually the train was moving, chugging laboriously away from Breslau. I knew we wouldn't be stopping for any more passengers.

As the day passed, we went through many stations, never stopping, barely slowing down. We saw many refugees standing on station platforms, looking disappointed when the train did not stop. My heart went out to them. Our spirits were soon buoyed by the light-hearted banter of a group of youngsters trying to cheer up the people in the compartment and to lighten the atmosphere of gloom. Some people remained shattered and downcast; nothing seemed to brighten their faces. For my part, I was glad to be on the move, notwithstanding the fact that I found standing up very tiring.

Suddenly everyone fell silent at the sound of distant bombs, and we felt the train slowing down. We were nowhere near a station. The bombs came closer and closer, and when the train finally pulled to a halt, there was widespread panic as everyone tried to get out of the train at once, and the whole process took ages. We ran to shelter in the woods at the bottom of the embankment.

Though frightening, it was actually wonderful to get out and stretch my legs and sit down on the cold carpet of pine needles beneath the trees. The quiet permanence of trees was comforting. There were three or four of these bombing raids during that day. Every time we all got out, ran for cover, and then got back on. One positive outcome of all this was that I was able to have a seat on my return to the train, thank God, for I was feeling so weary.

It was miraculous that the train was never actually hit, for bombs were strewn to the left and right of the tracks. On one occasion I was thrown several yards through the air, landing on soft grassy ground. I was winded for a few moments, my face muddy and my mouth and eyes full of dirt. Shocked and frightened, I stumbled up and away for cover and behind me I heard people crying and moaning.

When the bombers had gone, the injured were picked up and taken into the train. As far as I could make out, their wounds were not serious, and at the next station they were given help by the Red Cross. Not surprisingly, I found myself separated from my parents and Marion, who had ended up at the other end of our carriage after this raid.

It must have been about five o'clock in the evening, nearly dark, the last time we had to stop in this way. I was feeling quite exhausted by then, having had no food since breakfast, very little water, and not having slept the night before. My efforts to doze were not very successful. Once again the sound of aeroplanes and bombs stirred us into action and, once again, we all disembarked. I seemed to be in a sort of dream this time, not really awake, and I ended up being one of the last to leave the train. The bombs were close, the noise was appalling, and lights in the sky were flashing all around.

I tripped and went flying, throwing out my hands to break my fall and grazing them badly on the ground, twisting my ankle in the process. I must have cried out with the pain and when I tried to stand, it seemed more than I could manage and a dull despair swept over me. It would be easier just to lie down and let events take their course.

Suddenly two hands were helping me up, a voice entreating me to stand, and I looked up to see the elderly man who had invited us to come aboard the train. I made a monumental effort and, with his help, managed to hobble along to the shelter of the woods. I realised that he must have come back out of his safety to help me. Words seemed inadequate when I tried to thank him. He had appeared as a guardian angel twice now.

I find it difficult to express the feelings that swept through me when the full impact of this occurrence struck me – a mixture of gratitude and feeling blessed, of being somehow protected.

Night fell, the raids at last stopped and I managed to sleep. At dawn we arrived at Bautzen where everyone found their various pieces of luggage and disembarked. Families were reunited and people began to make their way into the town, many on foot, to look for somewhere to stay. We were fortunate in having friends in the town who knew we might be coming. They lived not far from the hospital.

At their comfortable home we were made very welcome by our friend, 'little woman', a nickname she had acquired when she was a guest in our house as a young girl and had become a part of our extended family. She stood just about five feet tall and spoke impeccable English. After a few hours of absolutely blissful care, food and good company, my father and I went for a stroll around the town moat. The evening was fine and I felt revitalised. Suddenly a pain gripped me, causing me to bend double and groan. Surely not . . . not a contraction; I was only seven months pregnant!

The pain went, but before long another followed, and soon it was obvious that, yes, indeed, the baby had decided, after twenty-four hours of being squeezed, jolted and thrown through the air, that it would come and take its chances outside the womb!

We walked to the hospital and at five o'clock the next morning I was delivered of a baby boy who weighed just four pounds. The nurses laughed when they heard this tiny being wailing in a high voice. My mother said he had a voice just like a silver bell. I was tired but happy to see his small perfection and decided to call him Tom.

I stayed at the hospital for a few days. My mother came to visit me, and on the second day, I noticed she was peering at me with a funny look on her face. I asked her what was the matter. She smiled distantly and dismissed my question. When I was discharged and was once again at the home of our friends, she told me why she had been peering at me in that odd way. She had been looking at my hair and noticed that it was crawling with lice. I had been aware that my scalp was itching, but had put this down to the fierce shampoo and even fiercer shampooing that the nurse had used on my hair. Mother proceeded to pour petrol on my hair, and on all our heads, and it stank for days after I washed it, but happily the bugs were gone.

It would have been good for all of us to have been able to stay at this 'home from home' for a few weeks, but after only two more days there my father told us that we'd have to be travelling on again. The Russians approached, inexorably pushing into Germany now, and were wreaking their vengeance on any German they came across.

Thanks to the people of the town who had all read about the arrival of the fleeing refugees and, in particular, of the premature birth of Tom, we were given a pram and lots of baby clothes, together with cards and presents expressing much compassion and sympathy. I was overwhelmed by their kindness. But the thought of another journey was daunting. What if the train were as full as the last one – where would a baby carriage go?

That evening, our last night in Bautzen, we heard bombing in the distance and soon afterwards saw the western sky illuminated as if by a gigantic bonfire. Poor, lovely Dresden in the distance was burning. Much of its ancient and exquisite architecture was destroyed in the conflagration that night.

We were able to catch a train headed for Ranis in Thuringia the next morning. Unfortunately, there was no way to get the pram inside the train and so I had to wedge it into place on the ledge at the end of the carriage. As the train began slowly moving out of the station, I was just about to lift Tom out of the pram and go inside the train when a group of people clambered past, down onto the concrete platform, pushing by us and dislodging the pram. I yelled, shocking those around me into action, and with their help was able to grab the pram, with Tom still inside, and pull it back to safety. After that, someone found a rope with which to tie the pram securely to the iron railings on the platform between the carriages, and I was able to go inside and take my seat in the carriage next to my parents and Marion, Tom now safely in my arms.

I was fully occupied with tending my new baby and, to make things worse, we all had diarrhoea. Thankfully, at one of the several Red Cross posts along the way we were given some opium to ease the symptoms. These posts dispensed some medicine and also food, providing an absolute lifeline for us travellers, The rest of the journey passed much more pleasantly, in a sort of dreamy haze, owing to the powerful effect of the drug. It certainly did the trick for our stomachs, and made other problems much more manageable!

Chapter 3

WHEN at last we arrived at the beautiful little town of Ranis in Thuringia, we had been travelling on and off for two days and were pleased to be once again in a safe haven. My parents had friends who lived in Ranis Castle and we made our way there. It was already full of people who, like us, had left Poland and East Germany behind and were going west. Since there was only room for my parents, it was suggested that our little family – Marion, Tom and I – could find lodgings at the home of a local tinsmith and his wife in the town.

After a bumpy trip in an old car down cobbled streets, I found myself in front of a small terraced house in the middle of the little town. As soon as I met the lovely couple who owned it, I knew we were in for a pleasant interlude, and hoped it might be a long one this time, for Fritz and Trudi were so full of warmth and welcome that we felt as if we were coming home. They took us up to two little rooms on the first floor, spotlessly clean and furnished with comfortable beds. Hot water appeared magically and I gave the children and myself a good wash; then we went down into the old-fashioned kitchen where a meal of freshly baked bread and soup awaited us, laid out simply on a solid oak table. A great fuss was made of the children, and I told my hosts about our journey while eating this delicious meal.

Tom was turning out to be a very good baby, in spite of his traumatic arrival into the world and his long journey on the train. Marion had been quiet and helpful all along – amazingly aware and resilient for a two-year-old, and a great help to me through these times. She responded happily to the loving attention of our hosts and was soon pottering around after Trudi, trying to help with the household chores, chatting away, full of excitement. We met the couple who lived upstairs later that evening, Martha and Max, a cobbler by trade, who soon became firm friends. For the time being, it felt as if we could relax.

My parents phoned Kay, my oldest sister, in Frankfurt and told her what had happened to us, and within two weeks she had come to join us, sharing one of my rooms.

About a month after our arrival, Hitler's death resulted in the signing of the peace treaty.* Kay and I were the only people on the streets the day the Americans came marching into Ranis. We knew that they were our liberators and were so relieved that we stood, tears running down our smiling faces, as we watched and listened to the welcome sound of spoken English. The townspeople peered out from behind closed curtains and thought we were quite mad. It took time for the other inhabitants to realise that these soldiers were not here to plunder and kill, that they were no longer the 'enemy'.

My father played a major part in bringing the townsfolk into contact with the soldiers. The American commandant had been told about Father's fluent English and of his political and cosmopolitan background and had immediately appointed him Liaison Officer. This pleased my father enormously and restored his sense of purpose. It was interesting to watch the gradual transformation of the people's attitude from suspicion to trust as he helped to reorganise the functioning of commerce in the town.

---

* On 7 May 1945 at 2.41, General Alfred Jodl, the representative of the German High Command, and Admiral Karl Dönitz, the designated head of the German State, signed the unconditional surrender of all German land, sea and air forces in Europe to the Allied Expeditionary Force, simultaneously to the Soviet Union.

My sister Kay was almost immediately employed by the US Military Government as secretary to the Governor.

Our lives were blessed while we were in Ranis, and I still feel grateful when remembering the folk of the town and their hospitality, in particular our friends in that cosy house where the children and I lived. Fritz made Tom a tin bath and Max the cobbler made Marion some pixie shoes which turned up at the toes. On warm spring days we could sit outside on lovely carved wooden benches in the tiny garden behind the house and there breathe in the lovely spring fragrances of narcissi and daffodils and all things beginning to grow again. We talked about everything under the sun and felt at ease with each other.

However, towards the end of our stay there, one of the American soldiers showed me some photographs he had taken of the concentration camp his unit had opened up. The images of mountains of skeletal dead bodies and pitiful barely-alive Jews were a terrible shock, and made me feel sick and horrified. We had heard of the camps and felt deep anguish in our hearts – had not so many of our friends 'disappeared'? But there was no way that we could conceive of the horrific reality of the camps and it was not until I saw the photographs that day that I grasped the extent of the crimes that had been committed within my country.

It was a sad day when Kay came up to my room with the news that the Yalta Agreement had now been drawn up and signed, which meant that this part of Germany would henceforth belong to the Russians. Kay would be going with the Military Government – she knew not where – and the most prudent thing my parents and I could do was to move on again westwards – our safety could no longer be guaranteed.

Kay had told our parents before telling me and she said that after a long silence, Father had looked at her and said no, he was not going to move on. He had had enough of running. He liked it here and here he would stay. I realised that it was up to me to persuade him to leave, at all costs. The Russians would not spare us now, any more than they would have spared us three months before.

The news troubled me deeply. I feared very much for my parents' lives if they stayed, and for myself with two small children to care for and another long journey ahead. I wanted and needed my parents' support and love. There was no time to lose. It was getting late in the day and I began the long climb up to the Castle. My parents had gone to bed and I stood beside the bed, pleading with Father, trying to persuade him to pack up and come with us. I got very emotional at times and didn't put my case forward very logically, but I felt absolutely convinced that I was right. My father sat up in his bed and looked at me sternly and said that, indeed, I should take the children away, and he would do what he could to assist our departure, but he was too tired to go himself and once again to have to begin a new life. In those few months in Ranis, he had become very settled. He felt needed and appreciated there.

For a moment I felt selfish, urging him to come with us. Was I just thinking of my wish to have their support? Perhaps they would be all right in a post-war situation with the Russians in power, now that the war was all but over. But, deep down, I felt that this was just not true. In turmoil, I walked back to the house and went straight to the garden where I sat down on a bench, put my head on my knees and cried.

My tears released the feelings of fear and frustration. I began to pray, opening my eyes to the magical surroundings where I had spent so many happy hours. I prayed out loud, over and over again, repeating, 'Dear God, please let my father understand and come with us.' How long did I pray? An hour? Two? The night was advancing and it had become very cold but I still sat there, sometimes with my eyes shut, sometimes open, concentrating on my prayer.

Gradually I was filled with a sense of peaceful purpose. I became aware that my friend Martha was standing quietly by the door of the house in her dressing gown and slippers. She had tears in her eyes and I stopped my praying. I asked her what was the matter. She came over and embraced me. She had been standing there for long time, adding her prayers to mine, she said, and the sadness of my predicament had made her feel like crying too. She cried openly now as she hugged me.

'Martha, it will be all right,' I said. 'I feel much more hopeful now. I have decided to try again.'

We sat down together with a hot drink and, encouraged by her support, as the sun was just beginning to lighten the darkened sky, I began the long trek once more up the hill to the Castle. My parents were fast asleep and I had to knock hard to rouse them. My father listened to me this time more receptively – what dreams had he dreamed? Then, suddenly, to my happy surprise, he jumped out of bed, looked at my mother with an expression I shall never forget and said, 'Grete, forgive me, I never asked you. Do you want to go?'

'Yes,' she said, 'I do, but I will stay with you whatever you decide to do.'

There was a poignant moment as he held her tightly for a long while, his decision obviously made, and I could feel their love for each other, and my mother's deep understanding of his dilemma. Resolutely, she got out of bed, got the suitcases out and said, 'Let's get on, then, and pack our things.'

This time I flew down the hill, all my weariness gone. I, too, had nothing else in my mind other than getting those suitcases packed and being gone.

Fritz and Trudi, sad as they were at seeing us leave them, helped with packing and brought us a large package with extra provisions for the journey. With warm embraces, we took our leave from these two lovely people.

Martha and Max were coming with us, and we were all packed by the time my parents arrived in a van driven by an American soldier. Father proudly showed us his parting present from the Military Governor who had become a good friend of his. It was a gun, a collector's piece, inlaid with ivory and silver – a real work of art. My father was delighted, and yet also sad to have had such a good relationship nipped in the bud. Sadly, later on he was made to relinquish this treasure to the military government in Kitzingen when they called for all firearms to be handed over.

Chapter 4

WE SET OFF in this van, the only vehicle that my father had been able to buy at short notice, along with merchandise that he had managed to acquire such as cigarettes, tobacco and cigars. These were to prove extremely valuable to us as they could be used to barter for food. The van was fully laden with five adults, two children, the baby carriage and as many of our possessions as it could hold. We planned to return later for the rest of our things.

Max was the only one among us who had the courage to attempt to drive the van; not one of us had ever driven before! I sat in front with him and held on to my seat as he lurched forward and promptly stalled the engine. It took him a while to get the hang of driving. It was a bizarre and hair-raising experience, but he stoically kept calm and quiet as he made many a bumpy start, crunched the gears and stalled over and over again. I was glad I was the only one who saw the near-misses when eventually we were actually travelling along the road. Some of the other drivers were as inexperienced as Max, it seemed. Much traffic was on the move, and we were lucky that we had someone unshakeable and courageous at the wheel.

As we passed through the American border point and into safe Allied territory, we asked what the situation was regarding the Russian movement. We were told that their arrival was expected that day. We soon came to a village where we found a family willing to put us up. Leaving my parents, the children and Martha there, Max and I returned to Ranis, hoping to be able to retrieve the rest of our belongings.

DENMARK
POLAND
GERMANY
Hamburg
Bremen
River Elbe
River Oder
River Weser
Bautzen
Welun
Breslau
Ranis
Prague
CZECHOSLOVAKIA
Kitzingen
River Danube
Reidenburg
Vienna
Munich
Zurich
AUSTRIA
SWITZ.

Once again we passed through the American border point and were warned that we had very little time. It was mid afternoon and the Russians were expected before the evening. At Ranis we loaded our extra clothes and other bits and pieces into the van and began the return journey. Little did we know that meanwhile the Russians had already erected their border point on the road and we would somehow have to get through this.

With trepidation we drove forward and were duly stopped by two Russian soldiers. They told us to go back – we could not cross the border. This was done in sign language with much gesticulation, their bare arms revealing rows of wrist watches. Threatening fingers pointed back towards Ranis.

We turned the van around and went back to the nearest village where we emptied the most important of our rescued belongings into a little hand cart which we were able to acquire. Then we changed our clothes, hoping the soldiers would not recognise us when we appeared again at the new border on foot. But they did, and were obviously angry. About a hundred yards down the road we could see the US border point and, as Max engaged in discussion with the Russians, I resolutely gave the hand cart a push with my foot and watched as it careered down the hill, seeming to know where it was going. As it rolled into the American post, I shouted, 'Please keep it safe for us!'

'OK!' was the shout back, 'Will do.'

Needless to say, this incensed the Russians and one of them, a threatening and dangerous expression on his face, pointed emphatically first at one of his watches, and then back down the road towards Ranis, saying, 'One minute or Siberia.'

Hastily, we turned and walked back down the road until we had rounded the corner out of sight. A small rocky hill stood between us and the American border post and was, we thought, out of view of the Russians. We decided to make an attempt to climb it with the hope of reaching freedom undetected. As we neared the top, firing began. I threw myself behind a rock against which bullets ricocheted in all directions. Max had gone ahead to work out our route, and as he turned to come to my aid, he saw that the two Russian soldiers who had stopped us were scrambling up the hill towards me. He yelled a warning, but it was too late. He did the only sensible thing he could do and hid himself. Before I knew what was happening, I was being kicked by heavy boots all over my body – in my face, in my stomach. I passed out.

Max told me later that a whistle from the soldiers' commanding officer had saved me from more than my seventeen broken teeth and multiple injuries. The soldiers went reluctantly back to their base, and later on, when night had fallen, Max came back for me with some of the Americans, and they carried me down to the American border point where I was given first aid.

I didn't recover consciousness until much later in the house where my parents were. A doctor had been fetched, a very kind old gentleman who predicted complications to come and probably inner haemorrhages. He gave me some injections and because of these, I remained blissfully unaware for some time, and even afterwards only in a daze.

Gradually I became aware that little Marion was also experiencing pain. The doctor had diagnosed scarlet fever and this had led to complications – middle ear infection. She cried incessantly. It tore at my heart, and my own pain was buried deep in the recesses of my subconscious.

I coped with the trauma of this experience as I had already done once before in my life and was to do again . . . I forgot it. Had I recalled the events clearly then, I might have been full of recriminations and regrets concerning my decision to go back and fetch our belongings when I had been warned of the possible dangers. Instead I was unaware of what had happened. I didn't mention my ordeal, I asked no questions about it and no one around me at the time talked of it either, until much later. But by then I could not relate to it consciously. It was a story about somebody else, somewhere else, some far away time.

Eventually, we arrived in Kitzingen, after what length of time I cannot now remember, and I've no idea how we travelled there. Martha and Max had gone towards Swabia where they had relatives, so we were once again a small family unit.

Two things happened in this town where we stayed for several months which have remained clear in my memory. The town of Kitzingen had been bombed and many of its houses destroyed but it was not, as some other towns we had seen, totally devastated. However, life had been severely disrupted, and food and medicine were in short supply. In fact, we arrived just before a quarantine was declared. Typhoid was spreading through the town. Marion received the obligatory inoculation against typhoid. Unfortunately, because hygiene standards were not all they could have been, she developed an abscess which made her little arm the size of two. I took her back to the hospital where she had received the inoculation, and the doctor said that it must be operated on at once. The nurse took Marion into the theatre, leaving me to sit in the waiting room. I sat down to wait, feeling confident that my daughter's condition would soon be alleviated. Until I heard an unearthly, chilling scream. I will never forget my feeling of helplessness at that moment. Something was very wrong indeed, and here was I, quite unable to comfort her in this time of fearful pain. When the nurse appeared with Marion, my poor child looked at me accusingly as she continued to wail piteously. Taking her into my arms, I demanded to know what had happened, what on earth had caused her such agony? The nurse was nearly as distressed as I, and explained to me that the doctor had been overwhelmed with grief. A direct hit on his house some weeks earlier had killed his wife and his four children. He had neglected to give my little Marion anaesthetic. Could I understand and forgive him?

Now, yes, I can sympathise with his situation and understand his lack of judgment under the circumstances. But at that time the look in my child's eyes and her heart-rending screams made me blind to this. The agony which had been branded onto my heart took a very long time to heal, and I felt that Marion blamed me for her ordeal. Indeed, I blamed myself, and it was years before I was able to forgive myself.

A short time after this my baby Tommy actually became a victim of typhoid. He was dreadfully ill. He had been crying all day and was getting weaker by the hour as I started out to see a doctor with him in the pram. When it was my turn, the doctor unwrapped his nappy and looked at him. He turned to me and said, 'There is no hope – you must get used to the idea that he has no chance of surviving. We have simply not got the medicines we need here, and even if we had, it is unlikely that he could be saved.'

I took Tommy out of the surgery, my head reeling with this dire prognosis, but deep within me my fighting spirit rose up and refused to believe this was true. I said to myself as if addressing the doctor, 'You cannot tell me that he will die. I won't let him. There must be something that can be done.' My baby's life was ebbing away. I went straight away to see another doctor a block away. Having examined him, he also came to the conclusion that there was no chance of his survival.

I went to see several doctors, carrying Tommy through the war-torn town, along streets lined with buildings that had been devastated and blasted by the bombing. In some places there were craters in the road and I became more and more dispirited all the while, as each doctor in turn pronounced the same morbid opinion – that there was no hope for my son.

Finally I came to the surgery of Dr Rheindorfer. By this time my tears were flowing freely and I was beginning to believe that the doctors must surely be right. This was to be my last call before I accepted what seemed to be the inevitable. This doctor was wonderfully kind and comforting. I calmed down immediately and stopped crying as I watched attentively his careful examination of my child.

After his examination, he said to me, 'Can you please just wait here for half an hour – I'm going to cycle down to a farm along the road and get something that could help him to get better.' As he spoke, he took me by the arm and led me back into the waiting room where he showed me to a comfortable chair. Mystified, I sat down and watched as he methodically put some leather straps around his trouser legs. Looking at my anxious face, he said, 'Don't worry, I won't be long.' He wheeled his bicycle out and cycled off down the road. Beginning to feel at ease at last, I cuddled Tommy, who stopped crying and finally went off to sleep, albeit fitfully, in my arms.

When Dr Rheindorfer came back, he produced six eggs and some apples from his pannier and gave them to me! Sitting down beside me, he instructed me to make a purée of the apples and to beat the egg yolk into it, then to feed Tommy one spoonful of this mixture every ten minutes. I was to continue this right through the night. His hand rested on mine as he gave me a warm smile and said, 'There is no reason why he should not recover completely.'

I hurried back to my lodgings with renewed hope, feeling very positive and immediately began to use this simple remedy to fight for my baby's life. It turned out that all the other doctors had been wrong. By the next morning 'Tiny Tom', as we then called him, was well on his way to a full recovery and my heart rejoiced. Dr Rheindorfer's knowledge of natural remedies, coupled with kindness and compassion, saved my baby's life. I also believe that my perseverance had paid off – 'Tiny Tom' is now a handsome man of six foot four.

Chapter 5

THE *next day Joan's parents came for the evening. I had met them on one occasion previously when I lived in New York and was happy to renew their acquaintance. Their warmth, their good-natured banter and ease reminded me very much of my own parents, as their love for each other has always been an inspiration to me.*

Ruth and Matthew were excited about their forthcoming golden wedding celebration which was happening the following week. The whole, quite numerous, family was to reunite at the magnificent Tower Restaurant where I was also invited to a luxurious dinner. I felt honoured indeed to be included in their close family circle, and I had been told about the stupendous views over the whole of Manhattan from the terrace of the Tower building. I couldn't wait to see it for myself.

Joan's parents were quite thrilled, too, about plans for a round-the-world trip which would include some time in New Zealand where I was born. As we spoke, I found myself thinking back to the early years of my life there until just after the end of the First World War when my father and all of us had been deported back to Germany. As German Consul, he had been a prisoner of war for several years in New Zealand. Ruth and Matthew's interest was aroused when they heard that I had lived there. Many of their questions I just could not answer, despite the countless descriptions, stories and photographs I could bring to mind. We children never seemed to tire of listening to such stories of my parents' time there and of looking at all the pictures. Though I was only small, the images came flooding back quite vividly.

When I was born, during the First World War, in Christchurch, New Zealand in May 1915, my parents called me Elfriede – the word 'Friede' was to help bring about *Frieden*, peace. How long they had to wait! Inge, the first-born, was already nine or ten years old when I was born and I think she must have taken to that new little baby that was me, as our relationship was always especially warm, in spite of, or perhaps because of, the fact that she was what was then referred to as 'mongoloid'.

Karl-Heinz, the second child, was from the start considered a thinker, making him at times the centre of attention and of everyone's amusement. He was five years my senior. One day as he was watching my mother sewing and sticking the needle or pins onto her dress over her chest, Karl-Heinz, who had observed her with fascination, said, 'So that's what you've got those cushions for.'!

Kay, or Käte-Liese, was three years older than myself. I looked up to her in every way, and it seemed to me impossible to become like her. I admired her and must have been a perfect pest, trying to win her attention. I realised that things which were easy for her and part of her nature were well-nigh unattainable for me. That terrible feeling of 'Why can't I be like Kay?' was unfortunately reinforced by the very words my mother used when puzzled by my often inexplicable and impulsive behaviour: 'Why can't you be like Kay – always even? You're either up in the clouds with joy or deep down in the dumps!'

Twin brothers were born in December 1916, Fritz and Paul. Paul didn't survive – he died six weeks later.

My parents went through a difficult time in New Zealand once the war had broken out. Many good friends suddenly did not 'know' them any more. Now they were the enemy, about whom they heard and read the most outlandish atrocities. But that made those rare friends, real ones, so much more precious. There was a dear young lady, a writer, Phyllis Hollow, who remained as devoted a friend and neighbour as ever, and over the years came to visit us in Leipzig on her European trips. There are others my mother often spoke of who truly supported her at a difficult time when my father was in a POW camp on Soames Island, off the New Zealand coast.

My mother was a tall and dignified woman. I think she had a special refined beauty and grace about her that attracted much interest. One day when she was riding into Christchurch on the tram – we lived in one of the suburbs, in Fendalton – a lady came up to her and said, 'Would you allow me to paint you?' They subsequently got talking and were soon friends. My mother suggested that she should speak with her husband first about the painting and invited the lady to the house. My father was thrilled by the idea because in the meantime they had learned that the lady was none other than the well known portraitist Elizabeth Kelly, and when she came to visit, he commissioned her to do the portrait.

Elizabeth Kelly captured all the dignity, the exquisite beauty of my mother – her dreamy, grey-blue eyes, the expression in her tranquil face of gentleness and wisdom, her hands resting in her lap. The painting will remain forever a great piece of art because the subject comes alive in a most pleasing way. That is exactly what I felt when I saw the painting again after many years, in Starnberg, Bavaria where my nephew Jost, my sister's only son, has given it pride of place in his lovely home.

In spite of her dreamy eyes, my mother was a practical, down-to-earth and no-nonsense woman. She instilled in people a sense of awe, of admiration without effort, without demand. People respected and accepted her authority happily and willingly. We called her 'the Queen'.

My father was not a dreamer by a long shot, but his personality was outgoing, generous, warm-hearted, of considerable height, and handsome – in short, charismatic. He was able to create an atmosphere of excitement and joy, of comfort and safety. His was a rare talent, of making people feel at home immediately in his presence.

They were a perfect match, two strong people, whole within themselves, and to the end of their lives, I could observe, when I had the great joy of being with them, a love deeply founded in respect and mutual understanding. I am not trying to say that their marriage was all a bed of roses. How could it be, with five children, two wars and endless struggles for survival? But it must have been love in the real sense, growing in depth and knowledge of each other over the years and through their battles and pain. It gave me an insight into what the word love really means.

My father was born in a beautiful old town in Schleswig Holstein, on the border with Denmark. He grew up there within a big, happy family, the youngest of six and one of three boys. His father died when he was still a teenager and his widowed mother sold up their house in Husum to settle in Leipzig with her two youngest children, Inge and Karl. It was in Leipzig that he met my mother. Inge, his sister, gifted with a delightful sense of humour, attended the Fröbel Institute, a teacher's training college with a Pestalozzi background. It seems to me now in retrospect that it was inevitable that these two interesting women, my mother Grete (Margarete) and Inge, who were studying at the same college, should be attracted to each other. Not only did they find that their ideas and philosophy of life were similar, but there was a kinship between them, equalled only by their resemblance in outer appearance. Both were tall and very attractive, with daring modern ideas; they condemned the corset and wore long, elegant flowing dresses, gathered under the bust, which later on became quite the fashion.

Their avant-garde outlook expressed itself in many other ways, trying to break through the stronghold of some of the prevalent Victorian attitudes in regard to education. Margarete's meeting with Karl, unavoidable, was one of the classical 'love at first sight' events. Not long after that fated meeting, however, an invitation arrived for Karl from his brother Henry to join him in New Zealand and make his fortune there. With hopes that he could indeed forge a secure future for himself and Grete, he accepted and sailed for New Zealand.

It was not long before he found work and earned his living. Single-mindedly he also began to study in the evenings and eventually earned a degree in accountancy and later on in law. He settled in Christchurch and finally worked up to a situation where he could open his own business. In the meantime letters went to and fro over the oceans. My mother, always eager to open my father's mind to the cultural education he had missed out on, sent him countless books: Goethe, Shakespeare and many others, contemporary and classical. Their letters were a life-line for both. Their love was so deep that ten years of waiting could not deter my mother, nor him, from their promise to wait till he could build a home and then bring her over to join him.

During the ten years of separation my father worked hard and also made many friends. With a chuckle, he reminisced about one occasion when he went on a hunting trip with some friends up into the mountains. In the hut where they stayed one night it was his turn to cook. Everyone insisted that he cook sauerkraut. He sent two men down to the village to get bread, butter, sugar and eggs. He fried the bread, soaked in eggs with sugar, in butter and everyone was happy to have finally eaten sauerkraut! When they eventually found out the truth, there was a raucous, good-natured battle and, of course, he never heard the end of it.

His personality, strong and forthright and peppered with the family trait of wit and humour, gained him respect and popularity. His name was suggested for the post of German Konsul for New Zealand, and he was given the appointment from the Kaiser und König of Germany. That must have been at the beginning of the new century.

My mother with my brother Fritz and myself, surrounded by the Hellfritz children. Devonport, nr. Auckland, 1921.

After the end of the First World War my father was released from the POW camp in Soames Island. The family – my parents and we five children – were to go back to Germany. A house on the beach at Brighton, near Auckland, on the North Island of New Zealand, was made available for us and another family of a similar size while we waited passage on a freighter, the *Otorama*. The months there remain vaguely in my memory as a period of happy independence on the beach, collecting shells, learning to swim and having much fun with the Hellfritzs' five children. We could pair off in perfect age groups.

Finally the *Otorama* arrived in Auckland harbour. My parents and the other couple had their hands full containing the unbearable thrill and anticipation of ten children, running around excitedly, losing and finding again one or the other item of their little pieces of luggage, accompanied by cries of woe or delight, jumping with joy, or feeling a happy bewilderment, as I was, as so often in a world of my own.

The ship seemed enormous; the water endless. Where were we going, and why? I wondered. The captain had given my mother and Mrs Hellfritz some valuable advice: to take lots of beads, colourful ribbons, hairpins and such like. He told them that when the ship stopped at Pitcairn Island they would come in handy to barter for fresh fruit like bananas, oranges and lots of other fruit we may never have tasted before. The two women had a successful shopping spree in the morning before the ship sailed, filling their baskets to the brim with all the odds and ends that proved later to be of such extraordinary value to the sea-faring families.

When the moment arrived to board the ship, I must have slipped into a kind of trance. The wonderful smell of tar, seaweed, paint, fish and other strange odours – a bouquet from a million and one sources – stimulated my imagination. The whiteness of it all wrapped me in a bright world of wonder. In later years, whenever I had the occasion to breathe in the air on a ship at anchor or at a port, the same miraculous magic transported me back to Auckland harbour, reliving a moment of bliss.

We never got tired of watching the dolphins following the ship on both sides, jumping into the air, outdoing each other as if aware of their admiring audience. The boat became one big adventure park for us. We seemed to swarm all over it like ants and into all corners, nooks and crannies, making friends with the crew, forgetting time and orders about it. My father, in his despair, had a brain wave. He thought of a brilliant way to round up this wild flock of children. In agreement with Mr Hellfritz and the captain, they had the sirens sounded, full blast at a piercing pitch, enough to awaken the dead. We were so terrified by the deafening noise that we flew from all directions immediately to our mothers' sides. There was a very satisfied and slightly smug smile on my father's face when, in later years, he recounted this story of his victory at restoring his authority.

When we finally approached Pitcairn Island my mother and Mrs Hellfritz got their baskets out and we waited for the islanders to come. They had seen the freighter approach and we saw them in the distance, like ants, clambering into their long canoes with outriggers and pulling out to sea. Each was manned by about eight men. Slowly we could make them out more and more clearly and we started to hear their song – a glorious blend of voices, tones and harmonies, getting louder and more moving every minute. It was this approaching spectacle that impressed itself deeply in my mind more than anything else on this voyage. Again I was under a spell, in another world. Their huge baskets were heaved up the rope ladders and were soon followed by dozens of smiling brown islanders who quickly found their way on board and began to barter their wares. The utter lusciousness of the fruit took our breath away. The fragrant smell of it all, the brilliant colours, the chatter, the barter and strange sounds were heady stuff. The natives seemed exceedingly pleased with the things my mother and Mrs Hellfritz had brought for them, and we children were ecstatic about the wonderful fruit. Having dealt with the freight for the island and received refreshments from the Captain the islanders left us, smiling broadly, revealing rows of gleaming white teeth in radiant faces. Still, to this day, I can see and feel in my mind's eye the beauty and splendour of this scene, of their song in the departing boats, slowly diminishing in size and sound.

After weeks with a view of endless watery-blue horizon and unforgettable sunsets, I was taken aback one day to look out from the deck and find a wall blocking my view. I looked around, confused and worried, and my father, who had been watching me and seemed always to understand and know about the world I lived in, took me in his arms and explained that we were in the

Panama Canal. With fascination we all watched the rising and sinking of the ship during the different stages it took to reach the level of the Caribbean. In Colon we dropped anchor once more to visit the embassy. There was fresh milk and vegetables for the children, which we so badly needed. To disembark, the sailors took us children, one by one, down a rope ladder. This is another experience indelibly printed into my memory. I was not at all afraid. Ben, a very nice sailor who had often carried me around on board ship and given me little sweet presents – in short, a special friend – held me safe and firmly. I was rapturous, thrilled almost beyond endurance, by the depth of the view of the tiny boat down below, rocking in the waves and myself suspended between heaven and water.

We reached the white, stately building of the embassy, surrounded by well-proportioned gardens, abounding in a riot of colourful, tropical flowers. We were delighted to feel firm ground beneath our feet. In the embassy they were ready for us. We were received like royalty and, for once, my mother said we behaved ourselves.

Refreshed and replete from all the nourishing delicacies which had been offered in plentiful and kind hospitality, we were now tired and ready to go back on board where the sailors once more carried us up on the rope-ladder. This time I was fast asleep. The sea voyage continued across the Atlantic, beating a path to the homeland I had as yet never seen.

In Leipzig we were received at the main station, the Hauptbahnhof, by my grandparents and aunts, of whom we had only heard in letters. Their enthusiastic and loving welcome made me feel familiar and happy immediately. My grandparents' home, where my two aunts also lived, was large enough to take another seven of us into its comforting embrace. In the meantime, my father was busy finding a new house for us.

Chapter 6

THE new house we moved into finally was covered in wisteria. It looked romantic and beautiful, and was huge. There were thirty rooms in the house. The hall was large, its walls panelled in oak. They displayed the trophies my father had collected in Australia and New Zealand, from the sword of a swordfish and the gaping jaws of sharks, with their layers of serrated teeth, to the beautifully woven marriage mat of a native tribe. Its edge was decorated with beautiful pink and golden feathers, rare feathers as each bird which had to be killed by the bridegroom-hunter had only one of them on each side of its throat. I often contemplated the cruelty of humankind while looking up at it. Hundreds of these birds had to be killed so that the bridegroom could marry his chosen bride with a mat showing his prowess.

The house had a large garden with little hills surrounding it. A small pavilion-like garden house held our garden furniture, looking out over the many trees – apple, pear and cherry trees – and beds and beds of flowers, mainly roses. Lilac was my favourite flower and there were numerous bushes of them in the garden. On my wedding day, my father brought in almost all the available lilac to fill the walls of the salon with a magnificent display, the perfume pervading the house.

My best friend was a linden tree on one of the little hills overlooking the wall and neighbourhood. I found a way to climb it and made a comfortable seat to sit on, up in between its lush branches. It was a place I cherished and where I could go when things got difficult. I felt an affinity with the tree, as if it were a

My sister Kay (left) and myself in 1925.

human being, only better. I dreamed there, cried there and made plans. In my own way, I set straight that which was awry, and dealt with many of the puzzles plaguing me, and many a time came there to alleviate a forlorn hope. Usually I emerged from there right as rain.

My sister and I had to lend a hand in the house. It was sometimes my duty to polish the beautiful parquet floor in the hall. This was made much easier when my father bought a polishing machine, but before that it was quite a job to get right onto your knees, and wax the polish with plenty of elbow grease. My mother impressed on us the importance of knowing, through experience, all the work to be done in the house before we had a right to delegate and let someone else do the job. This way we would also be a better judge. We learned to cook, to iron, to wash and sew, to clean and polish floors and pots and pans.

Both my parents set us an excellent example. Their way of treating our home help was always respectful and kind without allowing anyone to take advantage of their generosity. Mother and Father were good people without any real sense of class or race distinction, tendencies I have found regrettably often in my dealings with people since then. I remember the day when a lady visitor was admiring a particularly precious and lovely piece of Sèvres porcelain from my mother's beautiful china collection. She accidentally dropped it and it was no more. My mother's immediate concern was with the utter dismay of the lady, whom she assured of the unimportance of the matter. I knew that Mother had had great difficulty in acquiring that very piece and admired her for her presence of mind and her generous attitude and forbearance.

On another occasion, I overheard my father speaking with my older brother who was about eighteen at the time. They were talking about prostitutes. My brother passionately expressed his disgust with their activity on a street he had passed through. My father replied, 'We cannot, perhaps, always be a perfect gentleman in our lives, but we can keep in mind that we know precious little of why people become what they seem to be. Worlds of tragedies may lie behind them.' He added, 'If you show respect to everyone, you receive it. The thing to remember is that you remain true to yourself, whether you speak to a king, a pauper, or a whore.'

We enjoyed a very lively and happy family life. The large dinner table was a meeting place where the strictest attention was paid to good table manners and behaviour. Not infrequently one or the other of us children was sent out to eat in the kitchen. Maybe our elbows had slipped onto the table, or we might have interrupted someone speaking, or, horror of horrors, our fingernails might be dirty or our hands not properly washed. But the lively discussions, stimulated by my parents, gave us full scope to voice our opinions about anything that concerned us or what was happening in the world.

My parents gave us a lot of their time and care. They made birthdays, Christmas and Easter celebrations marvellously exciting. Weeks before Christmas we were busy, secretly creating presents. Christmas tree decorations were made in an atmosphere of anticipation, all of us sitting around a large table, painting, cutting and sewing, the aroma of drinking chocolate and pancakes drifting through the air. An Advent wreath was made too, before the month of December started, to be hung on completion under the chandelier in the lounge. The wreath had four candles which were lit, one by one, on each Sunday preceding Christmas Day, when the last would be lit.

Days before Christmas the door to the salon was locked. Behind it my parents would be tirelessly busy with all the preparations. The Christmas tree was usually about eight feet high and was always placed in a corner in front of a large mirror with a wide, intricate golden frame, almost as high as the tree. The long table through the middle of the room was gradually filled with presents, and each of us, including my grandparents and aunts, had their own space. The names were clearly indicated and on each place was one of those cheerfully decorated disposable bowls filled with nuts, sweets, biscuits and fruit. All this preparation went on behind closed doors and our anticipation often reached feverpoint.

When Christmas Eve finally arrived, there was still a lot to go through before the moment came when we were allowed in. First, we would all sit down to a delicious meal, usually goose or sometimes freshwater carp with all the trimmings tradition required. My father would quietly slip out after dinner to light the candles and to burn a few fir twigs in the Christmas room. In spite of the agony of waiting, all of the procedures, like the dinner and later the singing, were thoroughly enjoyed – an accepted ritual that belonged to the memorable celebration of Christmas.

When we finally walked through the door and beheld the

Christmas tree in its magical glory and glow, its many candles reflecting in the mirror in a myriad of images, it almost took our breath away. The room was a fairy-tale vision. The scent of the burning fir twigs mingled with the aroma from the flickering candles, the fruit and chocolates and marzipan, and filled the warm air with a delicate bouquet – the smell of real Christmas, never to be forgotten.

The tree, mighty, silent and glorious, spread its powerful magic over us children and the grown-ups alike. My mother would seat herself at the piano and begin to play the first of the four or five Christmas carols we always sang, ending with *'Stille Nacht'*. One of the carols contained the lines: *'Zwei Engel sind hereingetreten . . .'* (Two angels stepped into the room . . . no eye had seen them come. They go to the Christmas tree and pray, then turn around and go.) The first time I really understood those words, I could have sworn that I saw those two angels come in, kneel at the tree to pray and then silently leave. I was transported into another world. I never spoke about it. I would not have had the words, nor the courage, to expose my inner feelings to anyone, but the moment of awe, it seems, still lives within me. When an old school friend of mine sent me a gramophone record of all the old and lovely Christmas carols and I played it at Christmas, it was as if the memory of those long past days had tapped me on the shoulder. With a shiver and goosepimples all the way up my arms, I relived that moment. With a strange ache, mingled with joy, I saw again those two silent visitors in my mind's eye, returning to the wonder of childhood innocence.

As we sang, we children would inevitably roam with our eyes over the expanse of the table, laden with all the good things. Finally, as the last notes of *'Stille Nacht'* died in our ears, we were let loose to find our places and tear open the presents.

My mother established an English Reading Circle, a group of about six ladies. Well travelled and intellectually interested, they were all quite proficient in the English language. The ladies delighted in reading plays by George Bernard Shaw, William Shakespeare and others, each taking a part. We children, being usually only my younger brother and myself, were allowed or rather 'ordered' to the salon to greet the ladies. My mother was always anxious to educate us in the fine art of social poise. We did our best. My drawings and our other achievements were praised vociferously, which helped. But our eyes were inexorably drawn to the table on which the remnants of the petits-fours, éclairs, *windbeutel* (a cream-filled, mouth-watering pastry) and other heavenly delights stood. As soon as we were dismissed and the table had been cleared by the housemaid, we pounced on the left-overs with glee.

I wanted so much to please my mother by being more communicative, like my sister who could prattle along happily without any qualms and totally at ease. It was so very difficult for me to overcome my shyness, the sense of inadequacy and anxiety in the presence of many people. With my own age-group, I was at ease, even rather wild and boisterous, but in a social setting, particularly when small-talk seemed to be required, I invariably froze up, unable to overcome a sense of futility and embarrassment.

I remember in particular one of those dreaded social gatherings at home which filled me with a sense of anxiety. Several Australian couples, an English pair and some American gentlemen were invited and, once everyone had got to know each other, it seemed a lively party. I was watching the English lady who was talking to a young man in that unremittingly cheerful way that, even when I encounter it today, strangely puts a damper on my mood. Just then a lady from Adelaide, Mrs Shields, began speaking to me. I remember watching my sister nod and smile to her partner, uttering Ohs and Ahs and Really! and so forth. 'That's it!' I thought and gave all my attention to the lady speaking to me, saying 'Oh!', 'Really!' and 'My Word!' in all the right places. I developed a great proficiency of facial expression and it became a wonderful new game.

After the last guests had left, my mother took me aside, smiling happily. 'Mrs Shields told me she had the most interesting conversation with you,' she said. I felt just slightly ashamed but also elated. I had discovered a way to make her happy and to break through my resistance. True, it was a bit cynical, but it taught me not only how to overcome my social reluctance but also eventually to recognise the value of listening. I learned that there are very few people really interested in your own story. They seem far more intent on relating their own.

Soon after we had settled down in our new home, my parents registered me in the local elementary school, only ten minutes away. We children had developed a bad habit of mixing English and German words, a kind of pidgin English, from which my parents tried to cure us, without much success. I found it difficult therefore at first to understand and be understood by the other children at school. I did soon adapt, however, and even went a bit further. I learned the rather unmelodic local Saxon dialect to perfection which, at home, was looked upon with disdain. But I desperately wanted to be just like the others and get rid of the awful feeling of being different. It had at times made my awkward shyness almost unbearable. I would blush for any reason, good or bad or none at all, and in sheer panic my mind would sometimes blank out altogether

I adored our teacher, Herr Wolf, who at times took pity on me and restored my equilibrium by being very kind and reassuring. He told us the most wonderful stories which fired my imagination. His classes were, I suppose, the only ones where I could gain praise and shine. When we were asked to repeat the story he had told us the previous lesson, I was the only one who could recount every detail, only because I had followed his tale with such an intense interest, visualising everything vividly in my mind's eye as if it were a film.

Soon my parents found a private school, a most exclusive school called the Servier'sche Privatschule. I hated it with all my heart. Some of the 'dried-up spinster' teachers (my name for them) were so blatant in their preferences for certain groups of children that I felt more hopelessly left out than ever before. There was no redeeming, kindly soul to ease my unhappiness. The bullying from certain girls took on dangerous forms; on one occasion I was pushed down the stairs by a particularly nasty pupil, and fell forward against the girl in front of me. She fell onto the landing and broke her collar bone. It was most unfortunate for her. I was lucky enough to get away with a few bruises, but was also thoroughly intimidated by the girl who had pushed me. Her threats prevented me from standing up for myself. I was punished and degraded in front of the class by one of the teachers, cutting deeply into my already very vulnerable self-confidence. The one good thing I loved in that school, though, was the singing. Every morning before classes began, we sang a hymn. It immediately put me in a less fearful frame of mind.

I used to travel to school on the tram. It stopped about a block away from the school and I had to go through a tiny alley where a perfume factory was situated. The air in the lane was impregnated with, to me, the most heavenly scents. I used to savour these moments, although I was usually a bit late and had to run in order to get to school in time.

When the time came to enter High School, it was a tremendous relief. In the new, less hostile environment, I felt my spirits rise and began enjoying my school-days. The first couple of years went quite smoothly. My self-confidence began to flower and I made many good friends. Then, when I was about thirteen, something happened which changed all that.

It was at home, in our house. I was in my little study, doing

Max Klinger Schule, Leipzig 1930. The arrow points to me.

my homework and had just finished an essay for which, I now remember, I later received a prize. I looked up when the door opened and Jacko, the eighteen-year-old brother of my French friend Nini was ushered in, announced by Frau Lindner, our housekeeper. She had to go shopping now, she said, and disappeared. Nini and Jacko were the children of a French family who had rented part of our rather expansive house. He said, 'Nini invites you to come upstairs. She wants to show you her new doll, and we also have a big box of chocolates.'

'Half a minute,' I replied. 'I'll just finish the last sentence, and I'll come.'

I did that and then packed away my school things. I realised that I did not need to ask anyone as there was nobody else at home. I just left a note to say I was playing with Nini for Frau Lindner when she returned from shopping.

When we arrived upstairs, entering their very elegant lounge. I wondered where Nini was and asked Jacko, turning round to look at him. He was locking the door.

'What are you doing that for, Jacko?' I said, feeling suddenly uneasy. He made no reply, just took me quickly by the hand, led me to the large sofa and began to speak to me ever so softly. My apprehension increased and I tried to jump up from the sofa.

He started saying things to me in French, most of which I couldn't understand. All the time his hands were holding me down. I was in a state of panic by now, and his hands were beginning to hurt me. He started pulling down my skirt. I struggled violently and managed to jump off the sofa again. This time I succeeded and ran to the door, screaming, 'Let me go! I don't like it. I'll wait for Nini downstairs.' The door was locked, as I had noticed before, and there was no key.

It was then that Jacko got very fierce and excited. He got hold of me and, dragging me over to the sofa, he started taking down my knickers. I screamed as loud and wildly as I could, but obviously he had carefully chosen this moment when nobody was in the house to hear.

My screams remained unheard. The struggle between us was violent, but in the end, of course, I lost it. I'll never forget the terror as he stuffed a handkerchief into my mouth and tied my hands behind my back with a scarf. I had the sure feeling that I was going to die. All the time he was saying weird and threatening French words, increasing the horror of falling into an abyss.

I still shudder when I remember the devastation I felt when he then left me lying there. It was as if a deep black hole had opened and swallowed up my life in those moments. A heavy cloud descended on me and I could not transcend its darkness.

I could not possibly tell anyone about the awful thing that had happened, least of all my mother.

The next day at school I was still numb and in a state of shock, obviously not paying any attention to the teacher. From afar I heard my name spoken several times till I awoke to the fact that the teacher was speaking to me. When he came over and stood in front of me, I remember being totally paralysed. I could not open my mouth, I just looked at him with a feeling that now everything would come out. I would be punished and that was the end of the world. I wanted to become invisible and must have looked terrified. He studied my face and probably realised that something was wrong, because he suddenly changed his rather sharp tone and asked me gently, 'What's the matter?' A dam then broke inside me, and first silent tears began running down my face and then the pain and the horror released themselves in a torrent of weeping. The teacher could not get a word out of me and eventually sent me home with a note to my mother. This would have been a good moment to unload my heavy heart, but I was unable. My mother would never understand, I thought.

As time went on, the feeling that I had done something terribly wrong set in. Guilt filled me, along with a paralysing fear of being discovered. My concentration at school became extremely impaired. I could not think properly. My attention span gave teachers reason to complain. I began to feel harassed, haunted, persecuted. And I felt there was no one I could tell. All I felt I could do in order to hold off any intruders into my inner thoughts and feelings was to put up a wall of pretence and lies.

At school I was caught lying on several occasions. I felt I could not afford to admit anything about my ordeal. The wall of lies I built around myself protected me from intrusion. Eventually the pressure of all the fear, anger and deceit drove me to a state where all I wanted to do was forget it all since I couldn't deal with it in any way. My behaviour became extrovert in the extreme, wild and adventurous to a degree of recklessness. Foolhardiness would often get me into a tangle and my resulting impetuousness did not help. It was, I feel, the strength and courage of my despair that propelled me outwards and made me excel in sports and other areas where, it seemed, I could prove my excellence and that I was not a leper.

The dare-devil attitude persisted during my teens up to the age of about fifteen when I may have begun subconsciously to take revenge on men. I would lead them on, only to slam the door in their faces. It must have been very confusing for them.

My first great love at that age was a boy called Horst. We used to cycle through the nearby Rosenthal – the valley of roses. At night, lying in bed, I prayed that one day he would take my hand into his and then ask me to marry him. After several outings, cycling almost silently next to each other through the woods, we finally came up the Scherbelberg (mountain of shards) where he took out his Swiss pocket knife and carved a heart into the bark of a huge oak tree, already crowded with many similar declarations of love, and added our initials. And then he took my hand. Hand in hand we cycled along quite close to each other. It was sheer bliss. Without words, we enjoyed our deep understanding. But it was never to flourish into full-blown teenage love. Soon enough, when I was fifteen, dancing classes began to fill my mind and took me away from him. I could not lessen his despair. All my promises of eternal faithfulness could not convince him that I was not lost to him. Indeed, his premonitions were accurate. Thus, the frail and innocent first venture into the world of love came to a premature end without even a kiss. The intensity of feelings on both sides was such that still today, I remember them and the sweetness of it. Later, sadly, I learned he had been killed at the front in Russia.

Chapter 7

For many years before Hitler came to power my parents took us to the theatre, to the opera and to concerts at the Gewandhaus. Season tickets for four allowed each one of us to develop a taste for one or the other performance. Often heated discussions followed such outings and, very wisely, I thought, my parents remained in the background with their views in order to give us a chance to find our own preferences and opinions. Repeated exposure over the years to the sculptures and paintings of our museum on many Sunday mornings was of great value in developing a fine sense of judgment and appreciation of fine art.

This also went for religion. Both parents were Christians but they insisted that we should be able to make up our own minds when old enough to know. Our christening therefore took place when I was fourteen and my brother twelve and a half years old. The two elder children had already gone through theirs at the ages of fifteen and eighteen. I can appreciate the freedom my parents wanted to give us, and I am grateful to them. However, I think that at fourteen one is probably unprepared to make a true assessment of one's beliefs. I have to confess that my desire to be christened had more to do with the general anticipation in the classroom of the festival of confirmation and the lovely white dress that was part of it, than any great desire to become part of the Christian Church. The year of instruction before confirmation was a good experience, but my belief in God and Christ remained the same as before – deep and devout – and the prayers we learned as children were as valid then as before.

I think it must have been an incongruous sight, two such tall and lanky children standing next to the font, the water being dripped on their heads. It must have touched my grandmother's funny bone. She had an inimitable way of giggling silently, when her whole softly padded body began to shake and wobble. It was dreadfully contagious and my sister, who had the unfortunate habit of yawning as soon as she opened her mouth to sing, severely tested our willpower; to everyone's shock and dismay we were unable to hold back and burst out laughing and couldn't stop. The priest, undisturbed, looking from under his shaggy eyebrows with a tiny twinkle in his eyes, continued as if nothing was amiss.

Later, we were left to the tender mercies of my mother who desperately tried to scold us and then had to submit herself also to the hilarity of the situation. Everyone joined in. It was a wonderful, irreverent chorus of laughter which included the priest, Pfarrer Dietrich, a good friend of the family, after he had performed his duty so masterfully.

At fifteen, I still gave my mother headaches. I never wanted to wear a hat, and when she succeeded in persuading me to wear one, it mysteriously disappeared, forgotten in the tram, the theatre or elsewhere. She did have a hard time trying to give me some polish and teaching me to smile at my partner – in short, to become a lady. I think she never quite reached her goal. I was rather depressed about it because I thought my sister was the quintessence of a lady, and I should really be like her. That is, until one day at a ball where we were both invited by a charming Englishman and his friend. He said to me while we were dancing and talking, 'You are a real lady.' I must have looked at him with an expression of incredulity because he laughed and wanted to know why I did not seem to think so. 'Why don't you say this to my mother,' I said. 'She thinks I will never be a lady'.

'Oh, she is concerned for your manners, and rightly so. One has to begin early, but a *real* lady is born, and she can come from the poorest environment. It has more to do with her character and attitude, with her inner nobility, than with manners.' I looked surprised and with a tentatively resurrected ego, I said, 'In that case, good manners is not enough to be a lady? 'No,' he said, 'not enough. Many a harlot is disguised to the ignorant or superficial observer that way.' I was elated. Not everything was lost. One day I might succeed. He never really knew how much he had helped me that day to acquire some self-confidence and a certain assertiveness I really needed.

It seems to me now that my outwardly rather boisterous behaviour gave me a certain popularity, something I enjoyed; but underneath was a bottomless pit where the gained self-confidence seemed to seep away as fast as it appeared. I had a strange, indefinable fear of authority; I was still dreading to be 'discovered'. Sometimes I thought that everybody could see in my face what had happened to me. The vicious circle, a continuous roundabout of mistakes and omissions, of bad behaviour at times, and then lies, held me in a vice. I could not face admitting anything for fear of the consequences. It was a wondrous realisation and an escape from a trap when, years later, for the first time, I could quite happily confess to a minor or major transgression I had, on occasion, committed. I discovered that nothing life-threatening, nothing devastatingly crushing, would happen to me. In fact, it made me feel wonderful, clean and proud all at the same time, to have been able to expose my momentary error. I had truly broken the vicious circle.

There was a very lively flow of visitors to our house in Leipzig in those years. The Leipzig World Fair, the Muster Messe, attracted many international buyers and of course many tourists. Every year at that time the town was filled to capacity and more.

I remember my father telling us with a chuckle about an encounter on the Augustusplatz. An American had approached him and asked, 'Can you tell me where the Kristallpalast is,

My father, Leipzig, c. 1930.

please?' My father began to think, and when he looked up to give him the direction, the man burst out, saying. 'Another one of those bloody Krauts! Does no one speak English here?'

'I beg your pardon,' my father said in perfect English. 'Give me a chance!' The consternation and embarrassment of the American was such that apologies stumbled from his lips, and when my father said, 'I am a bloody Kraut, but I *do* speak English,' they began to laugh and ended up in the Ratskeller where Mr Morton, the American, and my father had a good meal together with a beer or two.

Many of my father's business friends came to stay with us during the fair which usually lasted a week, as I remember. I was also allowed out from school to work as an interpreter, earning myself the incredible and otherwise unattainable sum of a hundred Reichsmark. I always looked forward to that extremely tiring but wonderfully exciting work every year.

Eric Allen Poon, a Chinese businessman, came every year for many years and became a dear friend of the family, not just because he overwhelmed us with presents, never forgetting any one of us, but because of his kind, yet amusing and exquisitely dignified personality. I remember most the enormous silk shawls and pyjamas, thickly and intricately embroidered in beautiful colours and designs. I have never seen anything quite like them again. Today's Chinese ware cannot compare in any way to what we saw in those days. My mother was given rolls of pure, wild silk, of which endless blouses and dresses were made for us. Then there were dinner and tea-sets of the finest, most transparent porcelain.

My great love was a delightful, quite large piece of art, a fat Buddha, squatting comfortably on the back of a water buffalo. It was intricately carved in teak, every hair finely chiselled out. I called him my 'Tatzelwurm', and for the life of me I can't think why I named him thus. The name makes absolutely no sense at all. Eric Poon also brought us some fine pieces of art, beautifully carved in ivory, so tasteful in their refinement, which delighted us all. They opened a door for me to the exquisite and rich world of Chinese art and culture.

There were Australian visitors and, amongst others, people from India and Siam who stayed with us several times, in addition to the many British and American friends. Our house was open to all. There were often evenings filled with music, in particular when the pianists Eileen Joyce, of later great fame, and Marjorie Blackburn stayed with us. They were studying music at the Leipzig Conservatory under the famous teacher, Professor Powers. My older brother wanted to study there too, but my father was of the opinion that music as a means for breadwinning was useless. He wanted Karl Heinz to take over his export/import business eventually. Despite his great insight into so many things, he could not recognise that my brother was never going to be a good businessman. He was a brilliant mathematician and a superb musician – two things of seemingly different worlds yet in reality inextricably connected. He finally decided to make a compromise, suggested by my father, and studied to become an engineer. Until the war began, when he was drafted and eventually wounded, he worked for Dornier, Junkers and Messerschmidt, designing aeroplanes. He remained an unhappy man, though, almost bitter. He could not forgive our father for preventing him from fulfilling his deepest desire: to become a concert pianist. My heart went out to him, as he was the one I could understand and appreciate most. It was during his musical studies, when he would practise for several hours a day, that I learned the melodies of many classical pieces by heart. Unfortunately, I did not learn the names or composers of these pieces until much later in life.

My school reports improved gradually and my basically happy nature came to the surface. I became a member of the

Akademischer Sport Club (ASC) and played hockey with enthusiasm and won several prizes in light athletics and swimming. My days were filled and my life was exciting, with the telephone ringing incessantly – to the slight annoyance of the rest of the family. Calls came from admirers and friends and usually involved invitations to parties or to participate in school theatre productions for leading parts. Several times I played and danced in public performances and also took minor parts in plays at the Altes Theater (the old theatre), the latter giving my pocket-money a bit of a boost. I had a hard time not to neglect my school work, as I desperately wanted to become an actress. My parents did not agree with me. There would be no future in it for me, they said. Becoming an actress was tantamount to choosing a life of starvation. The Altes Theater offered me a scholarship, but I had to give up my fight.

My mother thought I should explore my other talent, that of drawing and painting and, as I seemed to have a special flair for fashion, she thought of apprenticing me to one of the finest haute-couture tailors, Leistenschneider. At the same time, I was to take evening classes at the Academy of Art for graphic and fashion design. I had been an apprentice at Leistenschneider's for about a year, hating every moment of it, when unexpected rescue came where I had least expected it. One day, I told my sister about the conversations of the other ladies at Leistenschneider's which disgusted me more than I could say, giving her some idea of the subjects and vocabulary. When she told my parents, in no time at all my apprenticeship was terminated, and I was allowed to take up art full-time.

After the last year at school, most of us went to a work-camp (*Arbeitsdienst*) for six months. I went to a place called Denkendorf, an old cloister, situated near Stuttgart and in a vantage point overlooking some of the most beautiful Swabian countryside. There were about fifty girls, between seventeen and nineteen years old. The idea was for us to become acquainted with hard work, and to receive training in the diverse aspects of housework.

From a male camp nearby, we received weekly all their soiled linen and other washing, to be washed and ironed and picked up again the following week. In groups of ten girls, we worked in the kitchen, the wash-house (no washing machines yet!), the ironing room, sewing room or doing the house-cleaning and making up the fires. But it was not all hard work. The two ladies in charge were exceptionally nice and we often made excursions into the lovely country surroundings, learning many old and new folk and popular songs.

As a whole, it was a valuable experience. I looked forward, as did the other girls in my room, to the wonderful parcels from home which we always shared, brightening up many of the rather dreary hours of the tread-mill.

Because I had become rather a sports enthusiast at home, I stole out every morning, an hour and a half before activities started, to run down the hill and up the other side. There was a tree, a linden tree, reminding me with a pang of home-sickness of the one in our garden, my close friend. It didn't take me long to climb it and sit in its branches. At that early hour the stillness of the valley, the haze and the fresh breeze were deeply reassuring, and it became a must for me to run there every day, anticipating that precious half hour of contemplation and total happiness and peace.

One day I spoke with one of the girls, who came from Königsberg (then East Prussia), and she told me that the captain of the Zeppelin was her uncle, Kapitän Lehmann. 'That's a coincidence,' I said, 'because Professor Dr Eckener, the engineer who built the Zeppelin, is an uncle of mine, once removed. He's a cousin of my father.' We were both thrilled about the discovery and I told her that I had received an invitation from Tante Go, Uncle Hugo Eckener's wife, to come and visit them. On our next free Saturday, we hitch-hiked to Friedrichshafen. Fortunately, Tante Go was most welcoming, although we had omitted to announce our visit. That had been a mistake, as we had missed Kapitän Lehmann and Uncle Hugo by two days. They had just departed in the Zeppelin to New York, Lakehurst. That was not the time when the tragic and terrifying accident happened – that still lay in the future.

Knut Eckener, their son, was very entertaining and took us out onto the lake, Lake Constance, in his sailing-boat. In spite of the shock, for me, of being hit on the head by the boom, we had a wonderful time. The next morning when we came down for breakfast, we each found a five-mark piece under our cups. Tante Go wanted us to take the train back to Denkendorf instead of thumbing our way again. After a serious discussion between Elizabeth and me as to whether to hang on to the five-mark piece or go by train, fortune resolved the matter. As we were walking along the road from the house, a car stopped to ask us directions, which we were able to give them. They were going where we wanted to go, and when we asked the very nice young couple if they could take us along, they said they would be delighted to do so. Although our cloister was slightly out of the way for them, they delivered us right to the door.

Once back in Leipzig, I was walking across the Augustusplatz one day. On my left was the magnificent building of the museum and in front, across the square, I could see the long building of the Leipzig University. Suddenly I realised that masses of people were running around me, so many and so fast that I had to run too, if I did not want to be run over. When I looked behind me, I saw the helmets of policemen, chasing the crowd, swinging their truncheons right and left. That gave me wings and I flew, as fast as I could, through the crowd, to the other side of the Augustusplatz. I realised then that it was a Communist demonstration the police were breaking up.

As a result of an intrigue directed by von Papen, Hitler had become Chancellor in a Nazi–Nationalist coalition in January 1933, and any opposition was rapidly suppressed. Nationalists were gradually removed from the Government and the Nazis were declared the only legal party in the country.

Around that time my father's very good friend, Ernst Schulze, Professor of Economics and Social Sciences at the University of Leipzig, dedicated several of his books to my father. As the content was directly opposed to the views of the Hitler regime, those books ended up, like so many, on the infamous book mountain in Berlin, being burned. Both Professor Schulze and my father were tried, convicted and sentenced to prison, Professor Schulze for disloyalty to the regime, and my father for collusion.

During the anxious and depressing period of waiting for the verdict to be carried out, we were suddenly immensely relieved, hardly believing our luck, when an amnesty was declared, following the sordid Röhm affair. My father and Professor Schulze were saved from a fate, the extent of which nobody at the time could have predicted. Now, however, in retrospect, we can readily assume that we would not have seen them alive again.

I cannot recall another amnesty during all those years of repression. This stroke of good fortune kept us on our toes. We were forewarned, and from then on conducted ourselves more than ever with the utmost care. Again, in another severe and perilous period of potential disaster, my father slipped through the net.

Dr Gördeler, Mayor of Leipzig at the time, was also a good friend of my father. One day, as I was helping to prepare the evening meal, the sound of Dr Gördeler's voice rose from my father's study. He was complaining bitterly. I heard him say, no, shout, 'They want me to tear down the statue of Mendelssohn in front of the Gewandhaus [famous Music Hall]. This I will *not* do!' He indeed refused to do so and, in the wake of his refusal, resigned as Mayor of the town by 1937. From then on, I think, he intensified his underground work, with the help of many, including my father and my sister Kay, who used to go over to his house during the night-hours to do his typing. Their home was quite near.

Gördeler then became representative of the Bosch Company, which took him far and wide in Europe and even to the USA. He used these opportunities to warn his associates of the dangers of Nazism. Unfortunately, his urgent hints and signals, his cautionings abroad to take note of the writing on the wall, were not heeded – a lamentable fact illustrating the indifference, or ignorance, of the outside world.

Tirelessly he prepared for the famous bomb-plot which was eventually carried out.* If the coup had been successful, he was to have taken on the post of Chancellor. In the disastrous failure of the plan to kill Hitler, the investigation following the assassination attempt brought to light several incriminating documents, including a list of members of his proposed future Cabinet. After a short trial, he was condemned to death by hanging, which took place in the Prinz Albrechtstrasse prison on 2 February 1945. I was happy to hear soon after that his family had succeeded in leaving the country, in itself a feat of ingenuity at the time.

During the trials which followed, everyone involved in the plot was condemned to death, and many, together with all of their family, annihilated. 'Sham trials', my sister's husband called them. The trials had to be attended by young lawyers. One of

---

* The attempt to assassinate Hitler took place on 20 July 1944. However, Count Klaus von Stauffenberg had not placed the briefcase, containing the bomb, near enough. It stood twelve feet away and only wounded Hitler. Count von Stauffenberg was shot in the courtyard of the War Ministry the same evening.

them was my brother-in-law. Every night, returning from a day at court, he was filled with disgust at the way the trials were being conducted. He vociferously vented his feelings of total disbelief and anger.

For all of us it was a time of tense anxiety and fear. Would my father's and sister's involvement come to light too? To our great relief, it became eventually apparent that Gördeler had destroyed a large amount of the notes of the early planning stages, including evidence of my father's and sister's part in the scheme.

Chapter 8

They were free and happy, the days in Berlin, when Klaus, then my fiancé, and I used to get together in my one-room flat, enjoying an evening meal which we had prepared together, or listening to a new gramophone record. We used to eat on a large refectory table which looked small in the enormous room. The house was one of those generously built, solid and palatial mansions of better times.

The year was 1938: a year of hard work and lots of fun for both of us. We had jobs we found interesting, as a springboard to better things later on, we hoped. Klaus was a very talented artist and worked for a film company, designing artwork such as titles and posters. My job was in a fashion house called 'Eva' on the Kurfürstendamm. Eva, the owner, was Jewish. Attractive, with beautiful green eyes, and full of fun, she was an inspiring personality. Her crazy sense of humour appealed to me enormously. It seemed we laughed about the same things. I was looking forward every day to going to work. I was employed there as a fashion designer but she called on me sometimes to help out as a model, in particular for one gown, only because she loved the way I made the voluminous, gorgeous champagne-coloured taffeta evening dress, swirl and rustle. I loved to do it – the magic of the dress and those subtle sounds immediately put me into a happy mood. I distinctly remember the day when Lil Dagover, a famous film star and a truly classic beauty, came to the studio. She wore her dark hair in a bun, deep in the nape of her neck. I had to show 'my' dress and did my bit. Lil Dagover was enchanted with the gown, tried it on and bought it. While she had it on, she swirled around the room, almost dancing, emulating some of my movements in a self-mocking, very funny way. She was enjoying herself and so were we, falling about with laughter.

At lunchtime I used to frequent a vegetarian restaurant about two blocks along the Kurfürstendamm, a wide, tree-lined, elegant avenue with high-class shops on either side. On 10 November 1938 I was heading towards the restaurant, totally unaware that I had just seen my employer for the last time, when I came upon a frightening scene. A small crowd of men were smashing shop windows, one of them full of crystal chandeliers. How apt the name 'Kristallnacht', given later to this tragedy.

Watching in disbelief, shaking my head, I was stopped and pushed by an SS man who addressed me with nasty and frightening threats. I walked on, shaking and boiling with ever-mounting fury. When I had crossed the Ku-damm and turned into Fasanenstrasse, I saw a group of men coming towards me, chasing a youngster of about seventeen or so, obviously Jewish, whose shirt was torn and bloodied. That was the moment when my fury reached explosion point, and uncontrollably I shouted and screamed abuse at these men with such unexpected power that they were totally dumbfounded and stood and stared at me. The youngster ran and I could see out of the corner of my eye that he had vanished round the corner.

Then, as if struck by lightning, I realised what I had done. This could mean my end and that of all my family. The shock of this terrible realisation was such that my heart sank into my boots and my bladder gave way. I was gradually aware that my new artificial silk stockings must be showing wide dark lines, flowing down into my shoes, revealing the most embarrassing fact that . . . I had wet my pants. Embarrassing, too, for those men who, I now felt sure, were hired to do the job. They were quite unable to cope with this. They just slowly slunk away into the Ku-damm and out of sight.

'Thank You, God,' I said, 'for such a brilliant way to get me out of this mess.' I felt it was just about the only thing that could have saved my life. I blessed my wet pants.

I learned later that during the next twenty-four hours thousands of Jews had their shop windows smashed and the contents looted. Homes and synagogues had been set alight and dozens of Jews killed, thousands arrested.

Klaus, who came to see me that afternoon, found me in a state of shock and devastation. It had all been too much. When I had returned to the salon, the windows and display had been smashed and the studio utterly ransacked. There was no sign of Eva. They had taken her away. Klaus then took me home to my parents in Leipzig where I could recover from what amounted to a nervous breakdown.

By the time I returned to Berlin, we had been married in Leipzig, in May 1939, and Klaus had got himself a much better job, as a cartoon animator and trick-film artist. His exceptional talent and delightful sense of humour took him soon to the top of the company. It also led to the filming of documentaries under his own direction. He was not able to enjoy his work for long, however, as he had to join a Navy training camp that summer, the last summer of comparative peace before war broke out. This prevented him joining my sister Kay and me on a white-water canoe trip down the River Drau and the Traun and other tributaries of the Danube. We had been invited on this adventure by Herbert Rittlinger, an internationally known author and photographer of several white-water canoe books.

It was an enchanted summer, and Klaus was able to join us for the last two weeks – a sort of honeymoon for us. Herbert and his lovely wife Avecle were old hands at this kind of life, canoeing in temperamental waters and camping in wild country, with unpredictable weather. But we were good pupils and our spirits rose every day, regardless of some rather wet lessons.

The book he wrote about that summer's adventures was entitled *Das Baldverlorene Paradis* (The Soon-Lost Paradise). When I last saw a copy, the publishers, Brockhaus, were still printing it after thirty-five years, and I was immensely pleased that so many people still wanted to buy it and share in those magical experiences. How prophetic the title, in view of what was to follow in my own life and indeed in the life of the world. For that glorious summer my world was full of joy and hope. I had married a truly remarkable and loving man and had felt at last totally happy.

However, on 3 September 1939, England and France declared war on Hitler's Germany. A year later, on 27 December 1940, my first child, Marion, was born in Leipzig. I was surrounded by my loving family.

A memory, gentle and sweet, comes back to me – quite insignificant, one could say, but it has stayed in my mind like a lovely fragrance. I was half asleep, keeping my eyes closed, when my father tiptoed into the room where I rested with the baby in the cot next to me. He glanced at me, satisfied that I was asleep. He stood in front of the cot, looking at the baby with an expression of total wonderment, almost awe. Then, gently and infinitely delicately, he lifted the baby's little hand to his lips, overcome by the miracle of a new life.

When I finally returned to Berlin with my little girl to our flat near the Lietzensee, I was happy and we enjoyed a time of family bliss. But not for long. Klaus was called up to the war after only a few months. Quite often we had discussed what I really wanted to do, and Klaus knew of my hope and desire to become an actress. He endorsed my plans wholeheartedly and suggested that I find a top drama school to register for an audition. It would keep me busy and interested while he was away. 'Will I pass?' I conjectured. But Klaus dismissed the thought with a wave of his hand. 'Of course you will,' was his answer.

Chapter 9

UNFORTUNATELY, Klaus's faith in my acting ability was not mirrored by that of the Nazi examiner who coldly told me, at my first audition, that for an actress I'd probably make a good secretary. I could still feel a silent fury rise up in me and I felt like making an angry retort to this pompous upright figure who held such an important role in the ever-increasing party of prejudice and pride. But in those days you did not answer back to a Nazi uniformed man, not if you wanted to remain a free person.

Another examiner at the audition, Werner Kraus, a much-loved and famous actor, was both sympathetic and encouraging. But for me to penetrate the halls of this well-respected acting school in Berlin, I needed the approval of both examiners – the one who was stern and caustic and the other warm and human.

Discouraged but not daunted, I sought out a brilliant Berlin actor to teach me privately and, under his excellent tutelage, I studied very hard under difficult circumstances. Marion was just a year old by then and although I had some help from different girls who assisted with the housework in exchange for lodging and a tiny wage, nevertheless it was a constant struggle. Sometimes I was so tired by the end of the day that I could have cried. At those times, the memory of the disapproving Nazi telling me to take up typing was usually enough to send the blood coursing through my body and revive my flagging spirits.

I played many diverse parts under the watchful eyes of my tutor, Herr Sanders. Sometimes I would wake up and wonder who I was that day. Together we covered three years' tuition, normally required at the acting school, in one hectic year. And in the spring of the following year (1943) I came once again under the gaze of the stern-faced Nazi and his quiet colleague, along with four other esteemed acting teachers from the school, to perform for the final exam which would give me the drama diploma I sought.

I strode onto the stage, probably looking more confident and relaxed than I felt, and began my performance. I wondered if anyone could see how apprehensive I really was. I played seven different scenes during the next forty-five minutes. Time seemed to stand still as I forgot myself and became totally immersed in the parts I played. The *pièce de resistance* was my final role.

No longer was I living in one of the most secretive and confused times in the history of my country. No, I was really Mary, Queen of Scots, in Schiller's famous play, pleading for my life at the hands of my sister Elizabeth three centuries ago in the faraway land of Britain. I finished the scene on my knees, emitting a long loud cry of anguish as I watched my sister coldly stride away.

I walked quickly to the back of the theatre where the other candidates were seated and, as I walked down the aisle, the applause rose up around me. I smiled with relief and felt the warm glow of success. I felt that I had surely passed.

Several other hopefuls were still to come. Altogether, one hundred and twenty young people had gone before the panel over the past five days and of those only twenty passed. Thankfully, my name was among them. What a relief! I noticed a smile on the face of the caustic-tongued Nazi as he read the remarks concerning my performance, and I cherished a secret smile of triumph for having, after all, achieved what I had wanted so much, and set out to do. In due course my diploma arrived. I was overjoyed.

Meanwhile the war continued around me, and bombing raids were a part of everyday life in Berlin. After completing my acting training, I found that there were very few acting positions available, and my unfortunate involvement with a young girl just out of school added new dimensions to the difficulties.

This girl, Else, just sixteen, had come to live with me as an au pair to help with housework and occasionally look after Marion. I knew one had to be discreet in those times. The fact that I had some very dear friends who happened to be Jews would have been obvious to this young girl who shared my flat. Unlike myself, Else was not very forthcoming about herself and her views. My natural instinct to trust and think the best of people had attributed this to her shyness and inexperience of life. It wasn't apparent that the girl had been heavily influenced by Nazi ideals and had been an enthusiastic member of Hitler's Youth Movement at school, although, looking back, I now realise that many girls and boys at that time were being more or less successfully indoctrinated into a creed which encouraged mistrust of one's fellow citizens and even family and friends.

One day my Jewish friend Ilse Simonson, whom I had known since my schooldays, came to visit, as she often did. This lovely, dignified and elegant lady was obliged to wear on her coat a yellow star, the degrading compulsory sign of her Jewishness. I laid her coat down on the trunk in the hallway and noticed Else looking wide-eyed and interested.

I had a strange feeling as I remembered other times when the girl's behaviour had given me cause for suspicion. As well as being tight-lipped and looking sulky much of the time, I had also noticed that little pieces of jewellery had gone missing. I had put it down to my own forgetfulness. I made a mental note to find out more about the girl's background.

A few days later, when Else was away for the weekend, I took the opportunity to look through the girl's belongings. It was a shock to discover what looked remarkably like a corner of one of my scarves just protruding from the chest of drawers. I opened the drawer, to find not only that scarf, but also many other pieces of clothing and jewellery that the girl had stolen in the short time she had lived with me. I was horrified, very disappointed and sad. I got quite angry to think that someone I had tried so hard to make comfortable and feel at home had betrayed me. I suppose I was rather inexperienced. It was a hard lesson to learn.

When Else returned from her weekend away, I dismissed her, expressing my hurt and anger. Tearfully, she packed the things that belonged to her and departed, saying, 'You'll be sorry, just wait and see.'

Else must have gone almost immediately to the Ministry of Theatre, a Nazi-Government organisation, and denounced me for my 'Jewish sympathies'. It became apparent after a while that I was on a blacklist. I went for several auditions and each time was turned down, which greatly puzzled and disappointed me. Eventually, one of the people who had auditioned me took me aside and told me that I was on a blacklist and could be sure now that there wasn't a chance of getting a job on the stage in this city.

The final straw from life in Berlin came in the autumn of 1943 when Klaus and I missed certain death by a day's grace. Klaus was home on leave. We had a week together before he had to return to his base in Greece. We spent a few happy days in our spacious flat overlooking the Lietzensee, the beautiful lake which was encircled by magnificent mansions where film stars and directors, artists and antiques dealers lived. We walked in the park by the lake on one of these precious days. Marion threw bits of bread to the ducks and Klaus's witty comments made me laugh as I hadn't done in ages. He had such a gift for mimicry.

In the days when I first knew him, in the years before the War, he lived in the family home on the outskirts of Leipzig next to a forest. People would often come to share the open hospitality of this welcoming house. He and his three brothers used to put on little skits which would render their visitors helpless with laughter with their quick repartee and incisive impersonations of popular figures of the time. Their mother, a brilliant pianist, would perform any of Beethoven's symphonies on request – she knew them all by heart – and the house was filled with her paintings. A very creative family. It was his father, though, who was the soul of the house: a brilliant journalist whose wit and fun brightened up every occasion. He was kind and gentle too and seemed to understand much more than he usually let on, loving and wise.

These happy days with Klaus were so refreshing after the depressing aftermath of the incident with Else. Klaus's company always made me feel carefree and young. We laughed so much that my sides ached and tears ran down my cheeks. For a brief sunny afternoon, walking beside the lake with my husband and child, the war seemed not to exist, and the future, filled with happiness, stretched out ahead. After the war, there seemed so much to look forward to and surely the war would be over soon, we thought.

On the last whole day of that precious week, Klaus had decided to help me finish some decorating in the flat which was on the ground floor of an elegant six-storey modern apartment building. We had spent the morning moving furniture out of our bedroom at the front of the house into the living room at the back, a room which overlooked a lush green garden and, beyond, the beautiful lake. Our bed fitted comfortably into one corner of the spacious room.

That night, exhausted from the exertions of moving all our things, and from wielding a paintbrush all day, I collapsed into bed beside Klaus. Marion was sleeping in her cot in the little room next door. I must have been asleep only a short while when suddenly I sat bolt upright, shaking and frightened.

'Klaus, something is happening. Wake up!'

My husband woke, rubbing his eyes and looking sleepy.

'What is it, Pucki? I can't hear anything.'

'I don't know. I just feel something is going to happen.'

Klaus stretched, not willing to give up his slumberous state for a premonition. 'Go back go sleep, darling. It's probably just a bad dream.' I ran out to Marion's cot, but she was fast asleep.

Perhaps Klaus had gone back to sleep, but I couldn't, not with this electric feeling that had awakened me still coursing through me. Suddenly sirens wailed. Marion began to cry and I took her out of her cot and brought her back to bed with me. Klaus was now fully awake beside me. Bombs exploded, first in the distance, then coming closer and closer, and then seemingly upon us. The sounds were so deafening that this time there was no doubt that we were in the firing line.

'Klaus, Klaus, it's happening. We're going to die!' I gasped, paralysed with fear. Holding Marion as if holding onto life itself, Klaus enwrapped us both with a warm, protective embrace.

'It's all right, Ellen, we're alive. We're going to be all right.' He kept repeating this over and over, rocking us in his arms, trembling himself. The loud and angry sounds of bombers and the whistle of fire bombs seemed to last forever, although in fact it can only have lasted a few minutes. Another sound, coming in waves, was the astonishing crescendo of walls of glass musically shattering and cascading far down onto the lawn below. Almost the entire back wall of the apartment building was one large window which had given each apartment its magnificent view of the lake. The chandelier in the living room swung madly like a wild pendulum, hitting the ceiling on both sides until it crashed onto the floor, making a horrendous noise and increasing the sense of doom I felt. Marion was shaking and quietly sobbing and we stroked her gently with reassuring words. Eventually, the noise of bombs and breaking glass subsided and, for a moment, it was almost quiet.

'Listen, no more bombs now.' Klaus raised his head and listened. True, the noise of planes had subsided into the distance, but presently the noises of people struggling to cope with the devastation – calling, wailing, and crying – rose from the debris and the elegant new apartment building had become a place of human horror and death.

At dawn we watched, speechless, as they carried eighteen bodies, wrapped in sheets and blankets, from the house next door and four from the top of our building. In the front room, where we had painted and slept the night before, two blocks of rock occupied the space where our bed had stood. They had been thrown through the air from the bomb-crater in the street outside. The tram-lines in the road below now seemed to reach out to heaven in a silent, grotesque cry of lament.

During the next few weeks I realised that I had been severely shaken by these happenings. The months and years of strain suddenly made me want to escape it all. As a result of the bombing raid, the residents from a higher floor, whose flat had been totally burned out, moved into my apartment with me. The Dutch Ambassador and his wife were friends of mine and I enjoyed their company, but I was now intensely conscious of the dangers involved in staying on in this confused and war-torn city. Klaus's departure back to the war zone left me feeling alone and vulnerable. It was time to go, to remove my baby and myself from Berlin. My friends gladly took over my flat.

Chapter 10

Within a month, Marion and I had undergone the long train trip to Welun, travelling through south-east Germany, then through Breslau, to reach this little Polish town where my parents had regrouped in an attempt to restructure their lives after Hitler's regime had destroyed my father's business.

Not long after our arrival, I received a letter inviting me to go to Muhlhausen, far away to the south-west of Leipzig, in the disputed parcel of land called Alsace-Lorraine (or Elsass-Lothringen, as it was known in German) in order to take up a post with the town theatre during the summer season there.

I was torn: Klaus was away in the Navy as a film reporter; little Marion was bonny and two and a half years old. My mother, seeing the look of excitement on my face as I read the letter aloud, said to me, 'Go, we will look after Marion. Go and take this opportunity, now that you have it. It may not come again and it will be good for you to have something to do to keep you from worrying too much about what is happening to Klaus. He can come to see you there when he has his next leave – it's in July, isn't it? And then, when you come back in September, you can help us get ready for winter. You know I love having Marion around. She makes me feel needed, and we have Trina to help me look after her now. You need to spread your wings a little while you're still young.'

I accepted the offer and was soon on my way. I had my first real acting job at last. As I alighted from the train on a bright June morning, I smiled as I found myself here on the platform at

Klaus at his camera aboard ship. 1942.

Muhlhausen, the pretty little town where life, during the day at any rate, went on almost as normal, or so it would seem. There were shortages, but perhaps a bit less than in a lot of places.

I found a nice hotel to stay in, but had to live mainly on bread and cheese for a few weeks, as my meagre resources didn't really allow for full board at the hotel. Daily I rehearsed with the cast I had been asked to join, a mixed and happy, lively little crew. The total involvement with their acting rubbed off onto me and I became immersed in my new job, which I greatly enjoyed.

Every few nights the air raid sirens would sound and everyone would descend into the cellar of the hotel. Then came anxious waiting for the all-clear sound, which didn't come for hours some nights. The hotel guests and other neighbours had to make themselves as comfortable as they could, and spend the hours as countless others were doing at the same time in other towns – in

Germany, Britain and France. I heard the coughs and snores, listened to a wealth of different accents, saw people from every walk of life. Always I seemed to find myself next to a person who wanted to talk, and that suited me. Most of the time, anyway. This way we all seemed to get quite close. We got to know much more about each other's lives than one would under normal circumstances. It was a bit like a kind of club.

Not long after I arrived in Mühlhausen, a lucky break occurred when one of the cast decided to leave the company to join her family in France, and she said that I could take on her flat – two rooms on the second floor of an old house about fifteen minutes' walk from the hotel.

During the next week, while I waited for the apartment to become vacant, I bought some bright, sunny material and made new curtains for the windows, looking forward to my move with growing excitement. I also made myself a new dress – blue and white striped silk. It cheered me up no end, and I felt it made me look very smart.

The day finally arrived and I was impatient to make the move into my new abode. I decided to take everything in one trip. I put on the new dress, took my two suitcases containing all my belongings, plus a shoulder bag full to bursting with food and a bottle of wine, and set off down the road. I walked over the main square of the town and along a beautiful avenue to my new home, walking past tall leafy trees which grew right along the street. When I arrived at the house, I staggered up the two flights of stairs, pausing to rest at the landing which had a window with a fantastic view over the roofs and chimneys of the town.

The rooms were hot and airless when I arrived, as the windows were shut, and I opened them full to let in a deliciously cool breeze. Then I set about unpacking my belongings, and felt a great sense of satisfaction when I'd finally finished hanging the yellow curtains and made up the bed. At that point I couldn't help but collapse on the bed and there I drifted away for a good hour.

I found myself remembering long hot summers in Christchurch, New Zealand, where I had been born. Perhaps it was the cool breeze coming through the window, just as it used to do through my window at Hallig, the home my father had built there and which was smothered in wisteria by the time I had arrived on the scene. Happy summers on the beach, watching the dolphins play; the sounds of my brothers and sisters laughing and swimming; picnics brought in a huge hamper, my beautiful mother clothed in long white dresses – she loved to dress the whole family in white – and sometimes joining them in the sea. A happy dream.

Almost hearing the sound of the sea, I thought of Klaus, out on the Mediterranean, facing unknown terrors of war as he captured the action on film. He was a pacifist at heart and had joined the Marines as a film reporter for the weekly news. Besides the regular film reports, he also filmed many situations conveying the cruelties of war and its horrors, with a fierce determination to capture the action exactly as it happened in order to show people the reality of war. He had made an award-winning film in 1943. He had been on a ship accompanying an oil tanker to Tobruk from Greece. The convoy had been attacked by British and Russian planes. The planes came flying over the ship, almost touching their masts. Everybody went below, sick and scared. All except Klaus, who remained stoically on deck – a solitary figure, with his camera whirring away, never forgetting name, number, rank etc., while shooting the whole incident. So low and close was one fighter attack that the face of the pilot in his cockpit and the name on the side of the plane were clearly visible and readable. When the film was shown in the weekly news programme at the cinema, the effect of the oncoming planes overhead was such that everybody instinctively ducked their heads.

What the general public had been 'spared' I had been invited to view privately. One of the tankers had been hit and the oil had ignited as it spread over a wide area on the sea. All around the tanker the sea was ablaze with the burning oil. From his vantage point aboard the Navy vessel, Klaus had filmed the whole horrific scene with anger and compassion, glued to the deck and compelled to film it all – people burning, jumping into the molten sea, their screams unheard in the din of many planes. He had witnessed the unimaginable terror of this inferno on the sea.

When Klaus had tried to talk about it with me later his voice had faltered and he shook with the memory of it. Although he had won the Knight's Cross for his bravery, and was hailed by critics as one of the most courageous film reporters the war had produced, he found it almost impossible to talk about the incident. It had left a very deep scar. He continued to go out and film events in the war scenario, hoping to convey to ordinary people the atmosphere of the most reprehensible side of human nature. One day, he felt, people would decide to put an end to all wars and perhaps this was the war to end all wars. I found the medal later, hidden away in the bottom of a suitcase.

Suddenly my dreams and reminiscences were shattered by the air-raid sirens, insistently screaming through the sleepy hot summer town.

'Oh no,' I groaned, still half asleep. 'Is this a dream, too?' Alas, no. The sirens continued to wail, relentlessly telling the citizens of the town to spring into action. Never before had the sirens gone in the afternoon.

Struggling against sleepiness, I sat up, slowly got off the bed, and said to myself, 'Ellen, you've got to pack up and go.'

Hardly believing myself, I got to work, quickly but calmly and methodically folding the clothes and placing them back into the suitcases I'd placed under the bed. I took the food from the cupboard, took down the stiff new curtains, unpegged my few bits of wet washing hanging on a line I'd strung across the kitchen sink and put everything back in their containers.

Then I carefully descended the two flights of stairs and began to walk back to the hotel and its welcoming cellar. As I reached the square, where five roads met, I stopped to rest, placing my cases down on the pavement, and I turned to look back in the direction from whence I came. Was I mad to pack everything and go? I could not quite understand why I had done all this.

As I turned and again faced in the direction of the hotel, I caught sight of three little silver birds flying towards the town. As they came nearer, it became clear that they were not birds at all but were indeed bomber planes shining in the sun, and they were approaching at great speed. I had never before seen these usually night-time visitors, and I could do nothing but watch, transfixed, as they separated and spread out over the town.

One of the planes kept on heading towards this part of the town, and a few seconds later the bombs whistled through the air and the dust clouds began to rise. The first bomb landed ahead of me and to my right, the next a bit closer and slightly more to the left. The plane was heading straight towards me. I could only watch, transfixed, as the dust clouds came closer and the bombs screamed at the peaceful town. 'It's going to be my turn to die now, no doubt about it,' I thought. The plane dropped another deadly load not a hundred yards from the square, then flew over me with a deafening roar.

I swivelled round and watched, horrified, as the fine old house I had just vacated became just another dust cloud as it crumbled and fell to the ground. For the second time in a few months, I saw the place I had just left ravaged and, this time, totally destroyed.

It was some time before I could move. I was rooted to the spot with the shock of this fearful experience. Eventually I was able to force myself to pick up my bags and walk on again down the street which led to the hotel, wondering what it was that had made me pack all my things with quiet determination. There was no time to think about it now. Silently I thanked God for having spared my life. Again.

As I struggled to get through the door into the cellar of the hotel, an enormous blast literally pushed me through the door and down the steps, tearing the back of my new silk dress, and I fell, to be caught by several people below.

The blast which had propelled me headlong into my chosen sanctuary had been caused by a bomb landing on the house next door, going halfway through the hotel at the same time. It crashed down right through to the cellar, and the wall between the two cellars fell, crushing several people on the hotel side, killing eight of them. On the other side almost all the sheltering citizens died under the enormous weight of tons of bricks and rubble. The cries, moans and anguished sobs of the people around me I will never forget. But I was still alive. 'Thank You,' I whispered again.

On our side of the cellar all was total chaos. Women were screaming, children wailing. Noise, dust, darkness, blood everywhere. In the dim light of a candle someone had lit I spotted Père Marcel, the French priest with whom I had often had long discussions about all manner of religious and other subjects. Here he was now calling for quiet and trying to calm down several women who clung to him and cried. I made my way across the crowded cellar to join him and the women and children who surrounded him. There was only one other man there, an invalid who sat quietly, as if stunned. With little discussion, the priest and I between us took care of those who needed it, dressing wounds, comforting crazed minds. We struggled to replace the mood of hysterical pandemonium with an atmosphere of purpose and action. Thank goodness we had the Red Cross box, a box of supplies and a big tank of water.

The citizens of Mühlhausen, previously almost untouched, had suffered a horrendous attack. My companions and I stayed in that cellar for most of two days, hardly sleeping, all trying to help each other cope with so much mental and physical pain and despair. We all thought that when, if ever, we emerged, there would be very little left of the hotel and the neighbouring buildings for a long way around. How right we were!

For eventually we were dug out and were rescued by masked men who gave us wet linen cloths to put over our mouths and noses. It was daytime, yet it was dark outside. The dust from the bombings still continued to settle, and it was impossible to breathe without a filter of some sort.

Life somehow went on and I was invited to share a flat belonging to one of the other actresses, Henrietta, a woman I enjoyed being with and who was easy-going and cheerful. She was the perfect tonic for me just now, once again suffering the after-effects of a fearsome, almost fatal experience.

July came at last. I had been cautiously looking forward to the time when Klaus would come for his leave – cautious, as all war wives were, lest he should never come. At last he was there, along with two of his film crew. They arrived with a motorcycle and a car which had a hole in its roof for Klaus to film through. We had a wonderful three days, the five of us, full of laughter and companionship, one of those times I shall never forget.

For this was the last time I would see him. Several months later, when I was back in Welun with my parents and Marion, knowing that I was carrying my second child, I had a telegram from his commanding officer telling me that he was missing in action between Lyon and Besançon, presumed dead.

Chapter 11

I WAS *a bit late getting to Martha's house in Brooklyn, one of those old brownstone buildings with a few steps leading up to the front door. From the other side of the street I could see that she was already waiting for me on the sidewalk. Strange feelings flooded me. The past. I always thought much of it was best forgotten, and forgotten much of it had been, or just buried? Now a shaft of light had illuminated a whole area, darkly hidden up till now. Martha, I thought, that good, wholesome and caring woman I suddenly remembered so well. We reached each other with open arms, in a wave of love and affection, as if it had been yesterday that we had parted.*

In her cosy sitting room, the smell of freshly ground and brewed coffee, mixed with that of German Apfel-Strudel, was enough to put me in a mood of luxurious contentment. I studied the room, taking in all the old and new of this American–European household, harmoniously existing side by side. The mellow soft stroke of the cuckoo clock made me turn to admire the elaborately carved reminder of German handicraft from the Black Forest, watching the little bird emerge and disappear with a rustle of its feathers. As my eyes rested on an old etching on the wall next to it, I thought, 'That, too, is the Black Forest!' I recognised a scene near Höchenschwand. Underneath, in fine calligraphy, was written 'Der Hirsch-Sprung' (the leap of the stag), a place where, according to legend, a stag, pursued by hunters, leapt across a valley to the safety of the other mountain side. When I had been there as a teenager with relatives, my imagination had been excited and I remembered my joy at thoughts of the stag's leap to freedom.

On the other wall my musing was arrested again by a painting, a lovely watercolour evoking a whole world of past bliss – the North Sea. Endless white sand-dunes with beach-grass, bent in the wind, the sea rolling in with white foam fringes, leaving traces of flotsam and lace, infinitely desirable shells and a multitude of unexpected wonderful treasures stranded there on the wet and darkened sand. Beach baskets, those familiar hooded wicker seats for two, throwing lengthy shadows across the sand. Without them beach life was unthinkable as they were good shelter against wind and weather. I was there, transported right into the picture, inhaling the fresh sea breeze and the myriad of other smells so typical of the sea.

I saw myself in the train, felt the almost unbearable excitement when we spotted the first glimpse of the sea, gleaned from the window as we approached our holiday destination.

I became aware, all of a sudden, of the expression on Martha's face. She had been watching me. It was a wistful look, and I wanted to say, 'A penny for your thoughts,' but she beat me to it.

'A penny for your thoughts, Ellen,' she said. I had to laugh, and admitted, 'I was far away, Martha. You seem to open up not only the memories we shared together, but your paintings, your home, seem to have started a landslide. I was back in my childhood again.'

'Ellen, tell me, where do you live now – you said in England? Are you married again? How are your two lovely children? Good heavens, they must be almost middle-aged by now! I have often wondered if you could survive all that without emotional scars, quite apart from the physical ones. What are you doing in New York? Oh, Ellen, a chance in a million brought us together again! After we left you, where did you go?'

'Hold it!' I exclaimed. 'Give me a break!' I had to laugh, out *loud this time. Her questions were tumbling out in an almost unstoppable flood.* 'Let me answer your questions one by one.

'Yes, I live in England and have for the past eleven years. I married Leslie nine years ago and that was the best thing I ever did.

'As you say, Martha, there were indeed many mental and physical scars. The beating I received from the Russians caused internal bleeding in more than one part of my body and as fast as the doctors repaired one, another seemed to go. I had a series of operations, each one taking its toll. The trauma of it all caused a loss of memory and some of those memories are only now emerging again.

Those first years after the war I don't really like to think of. I didn't particularly like myself then. At the end of our flight, we went to Kitzingen, where we stayed for quite some time, and then to Riedenburg near the Danube, where my sister Kay had arranged for us to live. She was posted there with the US Military Government as secretary to the Governor. It was good to live again in civilised circumstances.

My health was vulnerable and I did not know then just how long it would take to recover from the serious illnesses I suffered, like double pneumonia with pleurisy, which seemed determined to keep me down. I moved with my children from Riedenburg to Munich where the children began school. During one of the periods between illnesses I was able to find a job at Radio Munich, which was then controlled by the US American Occupational Army. I was cast as an English student travelling in the USA in a weekly series. Because of my unreliable state of health, they often recorded three episodes at a time. They were very good to me, picking me up at home in a big limousine and taking me home at the end of a day sometimes full of rehearsal and recording.

It was that work, the nice people, and the vitality and love of my children that kept me going. They themselves had been through so much, yet their innocence and the incredible capacity of children to be brave, to forget and to live for the moment, gave me constant support. I often thought that I would not be able to carry on if it weren't for my two wonderful children. I know I must be biased – all mothers are, I suppose – but both of them, at times, just bowled me over with a tiny remark, or a sudden little smile which spoke volumes, as if to convey, 'I know, Mummy, it's all right. I love you.' I tried not to show my grief, my struggle, but they must have felt my dilemma and instinctively, way beyond their years, gave me more of their concern than was good for them.

During their young days my physical condition was such that they could not be unaware that at times my survival was in question. Anxieties and an inevitable sense of abandonment must have deprived them of a sense of security they so desperately needed as they already had to deal with the fact that they had no father any more.

For many years in Munich and later I carried notebooks in my handbag, jotting down things of consequence – things I said, things others said and did, things I had to do – because I could not remember anything. And despite my memory props, I got into multitudinous scrapes, offended people. I felt that I was just no good and it was all my fault. My previous self was unreachable, my new self unrecognisable, and there was no memory connection to give me a lead. I did not like myself at all. It seems to me now that this was a structureless, me-less time. I felt I just had to muddle through, throwing myself unremittingly into situations without being able to judge, laying myself open to much criticism, malice and intrigue.

The nights unleashed the pressure in dreams, sobbing dreams. Quite regularly, for a long time, my children, Marion and Tom, sleeping in their own bedrooms, would be awoken and come to my bed, shaking me awake in the night to stop the crying. 'Why can't I stop this?' I thought. 'What am I doing to my children?'

It took time, years of conflict, mistakes and unrelenting knocks to my ego, my dignity and my pride, finally and slowly to regain my equilibrium. I spent quite a few years in a kind of confusion, a time I thought that was lost time. But it wasn't. I learnt a lot. That I know now.

Martha said with her ready and open sincerity, 'I was afraid that the result of what happened to you was going to be fatal. How did you make it through?'

'I almost didn't,' I said. 'I remember a dream from that time. The word "dream", though, doesn't seem to fit the experience. It was too vivid, and felt more real than any everyday happening. Since then I have read of others who had a similar experience. It is an extraordinary kind of dream which has a profound and lasting effect on the people who dream it. I feel easier speaking about it now, as I realise I am not the only one. There are many others who have confessed to the same unusual experience.'

In my dream, I was overwhelmed by the strange, intense luminosity of the images, the superclarity of the spoken words and the indescribable 'otherworldliness' of the sounds. The music, the view, the voice and the words, the meaning, the sounds all blended into one magic harmony: a symphony.

My dream started with a long, precarious flight through an endless tunnel. Far in the distance I could see a point of light gradually getting bigger until at last I had reached the brilliant opening. I drank in the breathtaking beauty of a bay, spreading out in front of me, with soft white sand and a sky as immense in its expanse as it was blue. Shimmering in the water were a myriad of hues of light and dark green, turquoise and indigo, dazzling the eye.

A voice, warm and sonorous, spoke: a voice I was going to hear again much later in another dream. I realised there were people near the opening, ready to help me through. Totally absorbed in the meaning of what was being said, an incredible sense of joy welled up in me. I was given answers to questions I had pursued all my life – burning questions: philosophical-intellectual and spiritual questions. Solutions to conflicts, doubts and hopes dropped into my consciousness like water assuaging unbearable thirst. The relief was such that no words in our vocabulary could do it justice. An understanding had spread through me, going far beyond the lamentable limits of logical perception. I had understood with body, mind and spirit all at once.

Then a tugging, insistent and urgent, finally pulled me back into the tunnel. In my deep regret, I thought, 'I must never, ever forget those answers!' My life took a long, deep breath. The restless, haunted feelings, for the time being, had vanished.

The next thing I knew was awakening in my bed, remembering vividly the scene at the end of the tunnel. The voice, the wonderful release at the revelations, the answers. But there I stopped. What *were* the answers? They had slipped away. What stayed with me, though, was the peace. Such peace as I had never known. It is true to say that it did not last for any great length of time, but every now and then it reappeared to remind me of what can be. I still tried to recapture the answers, but to no avail. However, a strangely certain feeling told me that those answers still lived within me. They now needed to be challenged, to be earned.

Martha was very quiet for a while, and then, as if in deep thought, she said, 'I have often wondered what happens when you die. I read Dr Moodie's book, "Life after Life" and he describes dreams clients told him. He recorded hundreds of them and in essence, they all seem to tell the same story, as you just now told me. There must be something to it. I do believe in a life after death, do you?'

'Oh yes, I do, more than ever after this dream. But at the time I didn't know I had had a brush with death.'

'What was the illness that could have been fatal?' Martha inquired.

'Frankly, my dear, I intensely dislike talking about it, but I suppose, after I told you about the dream, you have a right to know how it came about. You see, my teeth, which had been so badly battered by the Russian soldiers, had been repaired soon after the event but only temporarily. Many of them had to be pulled out and replaced by false teeth. Others had broken and eventually, when I could not live with the state of my teeth any longer, I went to a dentist in Munich who decided it was time to extract all of the seventeen teeth affected. It was only much later that I was told of the nickname he was given: "The Butcher".

'When I was in his surgery, I was given laughing gas. But as my state of health was poor in so far as my blood pressure was very low, the gas did not do what it was meant to do, not even make me laugh. But they thought I did laugh. I was strapped with strong leather belts to the chair in every conceivable way so that possible laughter movements would not interfere with the dentist's work. My cries, sounding weird, as my mouth was filled with all kinds of apparatus to keep it open, they took for laughter, and the efforts I made to force him to stop by rolling my eyes he did not notice. He never even looked at me.

'I went through hell. Mercifully, after several teeth had been pulled, I fainted and only woke up to see the number of teeth doubled on the windowsill.'

Martha looked at me, aghast. 'He never noticed you had fainted?'

'No,' I said, 'I was strapped up most efficiently. I will spare you the rest, but seventeen teeth were sitting on the windowsill when *they eventually removed the "torture belts" and I collapsed. My friends, who had been waiting to take me home, were quite shocked, but had no idea what had really happened. They put me to bed at home. It was evening, and I slept. Hence the dream. When I awoke the next morning I found I had developed a wide streak of pure white in my otherwise blonde head of hair.'*

I looked up and saw that Martha was quite shocked and shaking. As at Ranis, she had tears in her eyes. 'Oh, my dear compassionate Martha!' I thought. But before I could say anything, she exclaimed angrily, 'This man is a criminal! How could he be so insensitive? He should be in prison!'

'He did come to a sticky end, you know,' I said. 'One day I read in the paper that he had been murdered.'

'Did you ever regain your memory, Ellen?'

'Yes, to a great extent, little by little I recovered memories of what happened. But I still cannot get it all together, as if just a few pieces of the jigsaw had been mislaid. Actually, it was at a class reunion that many things began to come back. But that was much, much later.'

Chapter 12

A T *Martha's urging, I continued my story of life after the war.*

After another near-fatal illness with septicaemia, my physician in Munich strongly advised me to get away into a warmer climate, preferably the Mediterranean, where the sun and sea air could help me to relax and generally recover. Friends who had lived in Monaco for many years suggested that I follow his advice and go there. They could give me the right introductions and also found a little hotel where I could stay. With a letter from my doctor to a Monégasque colleague, I finally set off for a time of convalescence on the Mediterranean.

The illnesses had taken their toll and my weight had gone down to eighty pounds, which was quite low for my height of five foot ten. My parents had by this time established themselves in Giengen on Brenz, an old and lovely Swabian town where, incidentally, the Steiff animals, the famous toys, come from. My sister's parents-in-law lived there. Her father-in-law's machine plant had just begun to pick up again and he was instrumental in finding somewhere for my parents to live. They offered to have the children in the meantime and for as long as necessary, to give me a proper chance for recovery. The children were registered in a Waldorf boarding school in the neighbouring town of Heidenheim. On weekends they went to stay with their grandparents, and during the holidays they flew to Monaco which was immensely exciting for them. However, I hated leaving them behind.

With my parents after the war, 1950.

Recovery was slow. I was under constant observation by a doctor at the Pulmonary Unit in Monaco where it was discovered that one of my lungs had collapsed and the other was scarred. I needed to be careful, to take it easy and rest a lot. The doctor advised me to take daily exercises like walking, swimming and sun-bathing in moderation. So I enjoyed the beach and did a little swimming and sun-bathing, getting acquainted with people I met on the beach and liked. The colour of my skin slowly turned to a golden bronze and I was beginning to feel vitality returning. I still needed a daily mid-day nap and an early-to-bed routine at night.

I used to eat at a charming little restaurant called the Bordelaire, just opposite the Hotel Splendide where I was staying. The couple who owned it, Pierre and Françoise, were friendly and warm-hearted, their lively temperaments being quite infectious. They took to me in a protective sort of way; they felt they had to look after me. At that early stage my French was quite appalling, but their encouragement was constant and equalled only by their own wish for me to become more proficient in their language. With infinite politeness, they corrected my errors, although more often than not we were helpless with laughter over my sometimes hilarious mistakes which, I have to confess, were occasionally intentional to add to the merriment.

One day, after my evening meal, Pierre asked me if I would like them to show me the Moyenne Corniche and the view from its vantage point where one could overlook the coast far along the western bays. I jumped at the invitation and we started off at nightfall, first through the glittering town, past the Casino, the Hôtel de Paris and down along the harbour road and finally, leaving Monaco Castle on our left, high up on the rocky hill, back again through Monaco, and upwards, wending our way towards the Moyenne Corniche and Nice. The experience still lives bright and vivid in my mind. As you probably know, the

Moyenne Corniche is a road which winds its way along the coast, halfway up the mountain-side of the Alpes-Maritimes. Hence, *moyenne* (middle), as there is also a Basse Corniche, the low road, and a Haute Corniche, the high road.

Once on the Moyenne Corniche, we could see the strings of lights, blinking and sparkling in brilliant colours. The coastline was strung out with necklaces of lights, emphasising its bays, harbours and coves. What a sight! It took my breath away; I was overwhelmed. The sea was a deep emerald green and the night sky spread a phosphorescent glow of indigo over it all. I had never seen or imagined anything like it. 'Unbelievable,' I thought, looking at my two new friends with utter wonderment. Their faces seemed to say, 'Didn't we do well to bring you here!' A satisfaction and an echo in their gleaming eyes showed they were not immune to the splendour of the *heure bleue* either – not now and not ever. After many years of living in Monaco this first experience and the intense excitement I felt at the unforgettable view was never diminished. The impact remained as intense and impossible to get used to as a timeless piece of music, like perhaps Beethoven's 5th. I felt a strong desire to make this part of the world my home. 'This is where I want to live, and nowhere else,' I decided. And I did.

One evening during my convalescence, while having dinner at the Bordelaire as usual, I noticed two English gentlemen at a neighbouring table struggling with their negligible French in attempts to order a meal. Pierre, trying hard to make sense of what they said, finally came over to me, totally baffled, lifting his shoulders and spreading his arms in the inimitable way only a Frenchman can do. 'I can't make head or tail,' he said. 'Please come and help.' I was really glad that I had studied some French, apart from the happy lessons I had had from Pierre and Françoise. As I asked the Englishmen what it was they wanted to order, their relief was almost tangible. When they finally sorted out what they wanted with the help of my still somewhat lamentable French, they gratefully asked me to join them at their table. I agreed to join them, but asked them to come to my table instead. They were delighted and, after formal introductions, they came over. Soon we were carrying on a lively and stimulating conversation while they enjoyed their meal with gusto, helped along by one of Pierre's excellent Bordeaux wines. The inevitable question eventually came.

'What are you doing tonight, Lady Luck?' the shorter of the two asked me.

'Well, I usually go for a little walk, and then quite early to bed,' I said. I had already told them about my near-fatal illness and that I was here to recuperate; also that I was quite anxious to keep to the recommendations the doctors had impressed on me. But they were insistent.

'Couldn't you just for once accompany us to the Casino? Tomorrow you can catch up on your rest.'

I admitted that I had never been to the Casino. 'I am a total greenhorn,' I told them. 'I've never played at a roulette table or gambled anywhere else for that matter. I could not possibly be of any use to you.'

Undeterred, the taller of the two persisted. 'Won't you please be our magic charm, and play for us tonight?'

'Play for you?' The question surprised me.

He continued, 'You see! It is even better than we hoped. You'll bring us beginner's luck!' They looked at me with such whimsical charm that I could not resist.

'But what if I lose? You'll probably think up some devious and horrible punishment, and I'll have to run!'

'No, no,' he assured me, with a laugh. 'You are going to win for us, I know,' said the other one.

I had learned in the course of the meal that they were good friends. The shorter one was a handsome City businessman, the other a writer. He told me that he had been staying at a monastery in India for two years and his friend felt he needed a bit of 'the world' now, as he put it. I couldn't help thinking that the combination of these two from such widely differing worlds was slightly incongruous, but I later came to see what they had in common. They both had the most congenial sense of humour – wonderfully contagious and refreshing. I began to enjoy their company enormously.

I learned that Ron, the City tycoon, had been through a divorce a year previously and that Matthew, the writer, was a bachelor of unexpected and considerable means, having recently inherited a title attached to a large estate and a seat in the House of Lords. I kept thinking, 'How can someone so incredibly handsome' (he looked very much like Gregory Peck) 'be so gentle, so genuinely warm and unpretentious?' There again the contrast, the total lack of vanity in such a good-looking man, puzzled me. I suppose I was waiting to find out whether it was all a sham, a mask. However, time revealed no change at all. He just had this unassuming disposition. I did wonder if he had not grown through his spiritual searching.

Had I met Matthew at any other time in my life, I would have fallen in love with him at once, hopelessly. As it was, I was still quite battered from within, not ready at all for any emotional involvement, so I quietly took the opportunity by the horns and allowed myself to enjoy thoroughly what had come my way.

Our pact was made: I was to use the equivalent of £300 in francs, and make my bids on the roulette table. Anything over and above the £300 which I won would be shared between us.

They gave me time to stop over at the hotel to dress for the evening, while they strolled in the balmy evening air, exploring the little streets of the neighbourhood. I was really quite thrilled to be taken out by two such nice-looking and entertaining gentlemen. While I was getting ready and into my new light-green gossamer, chiffon dress, leaving bare one shoulder, the colour contrasting beautifully with my tan, I murmured to myself, 'I can use a bit of "world" myself,' at the same time wrapping a long, wide shawl of the same material around me.

My fragile ego was enjoying their 'Ahs' and 'Ohs' of admiration when I met them again in front of the restaurant where their splendid Rolls Royce was parked.

We drove down to the Casino, a five-minute drive, and I was introduced to the world of glitter and supreme elegance of many of the guests. I was totally fascinated by the tense faces behind façades of lack of interest, some with an expression of aloofness, quite blasé. Other faces held my interest, too, one in particular of an old lady with a dress and hat that must have belonged to the last century. There was a habit-bound sadness about her. She looked quite ordinary in a way, but there was something rather tragic surrounding her. She got up when she had no more chips in front of her and left her place to me. Later, we heard that she had once been a millionairess who had gambled away her wealth and was now on the Casino's 'welfare' list, where they gave her a certain number of chips every night to gamble and inevitably lose.

Now it was my turn. Feeling quite confident, I placed two chips on the red. They won. 'Good beginning,' I thought, and left them there with the winnings. They won again. Ron and Matthew were grinning at me when I took some of the winnings away and left the original two chips, which lost. 'OK,' I thought, 'I'll just play it by ear.' I lost another time, and after that it seemed I could do no wrong. I had won four times in a row and it was beginning to scare me. The £300 had risen to £3,000 and when I looked around at their faces, to convey that I wanted to stop, they agreed wholeheartedly.

There was hilarity and congratulations when we descended to the nightclub below to celebrate. The band was playing softly and elegant pairs were moving gracefully across the illuminated dance floor. My two gallant admirers insisted that I should have half of the win and I was not going to fight over it. I accepted with pleasure. Champagne and dancing in turn with each of them made it an unforgettable and enchanted evening. They were both quite concerned that for my sake we shouldn't stay up too late and took me back to my hotel.

The next day they called at the hotel to take me for a drive along the coast. We had lunch at the Chèvre d'Or in Eze and then went on to Nice. We had a swim in the Mediterranean and tea at one of the sidewalk cafés. Then they insisted that I should buy some new clothes with my winnings – something I had in mind to do already, but thought that sort of thing would bore them. How wrong I was! We found our way to one of those fabulous fashion houses in Cannes where, after much discussion and comparison, I bought a magnificent white dress, golden sandals, a new handbag and other accessories – all judged and enthusiastically approved by my two protectors, or rather benefactors.

Ten days of perfect bliss followed, where we discovered many of the cultural, historic, and other sensational attributes of that stretch of coast. I have never again laughed so much and so often. Over those ten days we dined in superbly elegant places like the Eden Roc and the Hôtel de Madrid, as well as enjoying immensely plain, wholesome French country cooking in a distant mountain bistro with splendid views across the Alpes Maritimes. We visited St Paul de Vence, Juan les Pins, the museums of famous expressionists; we climbed up to La Turbie, an old Roman settlement with remaining ruins, high up on a mountain overlooking Monte Carlo. We walked through olive groves, clambering up the wild mountain-side, resting now and then mainly for my sake, but also for the picnics Pierre and Françoise had prepared for us. I was introduced to Grasse, the village famous for its perfume where a myriad of flower fields stretched out in front of our eyes and invaded our nostrils with their intoxicating scents. I can smell it now.

I have a sun-and-fun-drenched picture in my mind, without blemish, or anything to take away the warm glow of a perfect holiday and a perfect friendship between three people. As it happened, each one of us needed space, a time to get away from what had occurred in our lives before. Happy and unencumbered like children, we enjoyed the moment. No conflicts of rivalry or anything else tainted our days. I have never again met two people so gallant, so merry and so witty. I have also never met them again, although we exchanged addresses and promises to write. It seems this was meant to be one of those brilliant moments in time and to remain unimpaired. I moved away and Ron and Matthew's lovely letters did not reach me until much later. Circumstances for me had changed considerably and my answer, delayed as it was, came back with the line, 'No longer at this address'.

Chapter 13

As time went by, it became obvious that the climate on the Mediterranean was speeding my physical and psychological recovery. One day, as I went for my monthly examination at the Clinic, the doctor exclaimed with utter surprise, 'Look! This picture shows . . . Come and have a look . . . your left lung is beginning to inflate again. Congratulations!' 'Great,' I thought, 'I will and must continue with the breathing exercises Vassilka taught me.' Vassilka had become a friend. We had met on the beach. She was a singer at the Metropolitan Opera in New York. 'These exercises are yoga exercises,' she had told me. 'They will help you to regain your full lung power if you do them religiously every day, mornings and evenings.' It was no longer than three months later that my collapsed lung began to function again, sufficiently to make me feel stronger and more at ease.

At that time I also met an Englishman who had lived in Monaco for a long time and had a business licence. We formed a partnership. I designed scarves which were then printed in Lyon onto exquisite silk. Bob was the salesman and took care of the production side of the company. I took charge of all artistic decisions. On the side, I was also contracted by a German and a Swiss manufacturing company to design handkerchiefs. It was great fun for me, especially since until then my self-esteem had been so low. It was a surprise and a thrill to see the immediate success of my scarves. It was also a kind of stepping-stone for me as, much later in Milan, I was able to pick up where I had left off and continue designing and selling my scarves.

Our business in Monaco expanded and, during our work together, Bob and I fell in love with each other. One would think that this was an ideal situation, but no. I soon found that I was still too vulnerable for this kind of relationship, and it became apparent that again I had trapped myself in an impossible situation. Bob had a very powerful personality. His eyes were a luminous blue and his shock of white hair contrasted with his dark all-year-round tan. He had a hypnotic effect on me. A brilliant wit, sharp and merciless at times, he certainly was stimulating to be with. He had been a journalist for the London *Times*, reporting on life in Hollywood and its stars. He had lived there for many years until he married and came to live in Monte Carlo. It was a tragic event in his life and his sadness about the early death of his wife from cancer that opened up my heart to him. Shortly before we met, he had sold his villa, a splendid place right down on the shores of the Mediterranean, because it held too many sad memories.

It became obvious after a while that I had really not recovered my inner stability. I was quite unable to defend myself against his incredible jealousy and possessiveness. In this relationship I felt I was slowly being blotted out as a person and my unhappiness increased. It was only through outside help that I could finally extricate myself from this stronghold.

Phoebe, a dear young friend and a live-wire too, came to see me one day. Bob had flown to England the day before and would be away for a week. I was breathing more freely. We went to our favourite restaurant, the Costa Rica, on the Boulevard des Moulins. There Phoebe actually begged me to get out of this relationship; to get it into my head that I must escape, that I *could* escape from being completely subjugated before it was too late. It seems I needed this broadside volley. She was totally convincing.

She even had a ready-made plan as to how to go about it. A mutual friend, the director of a hotel in Nice, had agreed to 'stand in' as my fiancé. She reasoned that it would be the only method by which Bob would let go of me. I could see her point and immediately sent a letter to London, telling him that I had had a change of heart and was now engaged to a man I had known before I met him. As predicted, the ruse worked. Since the engagement was only nominal, nothing else had changed other than that I had liberated myself from a stranglehold, and was now out of a job. I moved my designs and scarves out of our office and felt that the sacrifice of a good business was worth the liberty I had gained. I was very grateful to Phoebe that she had gone to such lengths to truly stand by me at this time in my life when I just couldn't handle the situation myself.

Soon after I had regained my freedom from Bob another serious operation was necessary, curtailing once again my tenuous hold on recovery. This took place while I stayed with my parents near Ulm. My joy at my reunion with Marion and Tom was dampened by the fact that the illnesses just never seemed to be able to leave me. I remember their anxious faces by my bedside in the hospital and I thought, 'Oh, God, they're thinking again that I'm going to die.'

Once more I returned to Monaco to my cosy little apartment. It wasn't too long before I recovered sufficiently to take up my design work again. My flat could house the three of us comfortably, the children and me, when they came for their holidays. It was situated on a hill, leading up from the Place des Moulins. Lipa, a sculptor, and his lovely wife Lore with their little son Pierre, were my immediate neighbours. They lived in a fairy-tale, romantic little house. At the bottom of their garden which bordered on mine, was a pergola-like garden house, thickly covered with trailing vines. We all spent many happy hours there in lighthearted talk or sometimes in serious discussions, putting the world to rights. My visual memory, so much stronger than my aural one, can conjure up every captivating moment in that magic little garden house – all of us sitting around a table covered with a bright yellow tablecloth, the evening sun filtering through the leaves, their shadows playfully oscillating over us all. There was always a rich fare of delicious snacks and sometimes a *terrine*, a treat we called 'Soupe à la Lore'. It was a dish full of delectable surprises for the discerning, and that we were. All of it was spread out to please the eye, and our palate of course; the glasses, filled with the wine of the region, occasionally lit up with the reflecting sparkle from a last ray of sunlight. The memory of those evenings in the afterglow of a hot summer's day and in the company of dear friends, when we enjoyed every moment in the cool and gentle breeze of the impending night, is precious to me. In such warm and congenial company, I started to make a steady recovery.

Some time before this I had met the director of the Hotel de Paris and when I approached him about Lipa, to see if he would give permission for an exhibition of his work, he was very agreeable to the idea. It was in this exhibition that Lipa finally came out of relative obscurity when the art world became aware of his rare talent.

Lipa worked mainly with olive wood, sometimes thousands of years old. He was a lovable man of few words, gentle and always ready to help when needed. Lore gave him all the support he needed to concentrate on his art. This new and well-earned success meant he could finally fulfil his vision of building his own house which he did in the hills above Nice, in the Alpes Maritimes. It was situated amongst olive groves, on top of a hill. The house itself looked like a sculpture, architecturally sound in spite of the total abandonment of orthodox rules. The inside was one warm welcome, almost like an embrace: comfortable, easy on the eye and practical. The enormous table standing in front of a vast window, surrounded by old chairs, was the place where we enjoyed many a splendid meal prepared by everyone present under the deft guidance of Lore.

Moving around the lower and upper floors, one could marvel at Lipa's original way of displaying his sculptures. One's vision was constantly surprised and enchanted every now and then, when turning a corner or looking through an opening, by Lipa's elegant and arresting work. The sculptures were of stunning simplicity, the intricate flowing lines of the wood-grain forming an intrinsic part of the overall design. Each piece of art was dramatically yet organically part of its surrounding and in complete harmony with the house. Stopping in front of one of Lipa's tall sculptures, one could not resist the temptation to stretch out one's hand to feel the softness of the form, the warmth and glow of the wood. His Eagle, a large piece bought by the Aga Khan from the exhibition at the Hôtel de Paris, was a particularly brilliant example of his genius. Not only was Lipa an outstanding artist but also an exceptional human being. When he passed on, too young, the world lost a giant of the art-world.

Next to Lipa and Lore, I formed another lasting friendship in Kiki, the Marquise de Suarez d'Almeida. I met Kiki at the Larvotto, one of the beaches on the Monte Carlo seaside where we both used to go with our children. Kiki had seven. Marion and Tom had made friends with them long before Kiki and I met. One day when, just by chance, we were sitting next to each other at the snack-bar, having a sandwich, our children spotted us and came crowding around us, all talking at the same time. They were thrilled to see us together.

We saw a lot of each other during the summers when they came down from Paris and my children were with me on their holidays. Their apartment was situated high above the Monte Carlo harbour where, in those early days, my children and I enjoyed Kiki's hospitality at wonderful dinners and lunches which their Moroccan housekeeper prepared. The huge table on the terrace, from which one could enjoy a stupendous view over the harbour and all of Monte Carlo, easily accommodated ten people and the lively conversation never stopped.

Kiki had fascinated me from the start. Elegant in an understated way, but more so because of her very special charm, a combination of disarming honesty and sharp intelligence, she was completely natural. We became friends immediately. The way she dealt with her seven children was a delightful study in how you can achieve discipline and authority without pain, and make them feel proud and happy about it to boot. I was captivated. She had a way of creating laughter and fun with the children and they adored her. Kiki had withstood many hard blows to her inner and outer security, to her pride and general equilibrium. Adolphe de Carayon, her husband, had died when their six children were quite young. The struggle to bring them up on her own had been a soul-searching and testing task, to say the least.

It was her common sense and an innate sense of humour which often helped her to turn a bad situation into at least a constructive one, if not even into a positively good one.

Then her life took a turn for the better, giving her new happiness and fulfilment, when she married again. Henri, Marquis de Suarez d'Almeyda was a widower who brought his young daughter Chantal into their marriage.

When I first met Kiki at the Larvotto, she had been married to Henri for a while. Dolky, her eldest daughter, tall, slim and beautiful, had married at an early age Sacha-Xavier, Comte de Montbel. She liked to spend her holidays with the family in Monte Carlo, while Kiki's two sons, Boby and Phillippe de Carayon, both students, were enjoying independent holidays. The other girls: Beatrice, Chantal and Florence de Carayon, and Chantal (Kalou) de Suarez d'Almeyda, together with my two Wild Indians Marion and Tom, made up a lively, incredibly healthy and beautiful young crowd – dashing in and out of the water and playing in the sun. They were happy days!

It was only after my return from New York thirteen years after Monte Carlo that we met again. I remember vividly that affectionate reunion when I answered her invitation to visit her in Paris. I was standing in front of the door to her apartment, ringing the bell and thinking with a multitude of mixed feelings: 'Will we recognise each other?' 'Will it, perhaps, be a dreadful disappointment?'

When the door opened, there was Kiki – unchanged, smiling, but with a wistful expression in her eyes, elegant, natural and enthusiastic as ever. She embraced me with genuine joy of seeing me again. With her old warmth and charm she dissolved all my tiny apprehensions. The closeness was still there, as if time had stood still for thirteen years.

I enjoyed several days in her comfortable and beautiful apartment, when I learned during our long talks of all that had happened during those years and that her husband had died. She was, once again, on her own. Now I could translate the slight shadow behind her smile. I am happy now that I followed Kiki's invitations then and spent several sun-filled summers with the whole, now considerably enlarged, family at Terraqueuse, their chateau north of Toulouse. Again, I was able to enjoy the extraordinary sense of togetherness of this family. Kiki's children and grandchildren swarmed over the lovely grounds of the chateau, the swimming-pool with the tennis court next to it being the centre of attraction. Some of Kiki's children were now married and parents themselves and the number of her grandchildren was continually growing. The whole family met, in a unique tradition of reunion, every summer during the holidays, as well as on other festive occasions like Easter, Christmas or weddings, at Terraqueuse. Kiki, the creator of harmony, beauty and comfort, lovingly organised and directed the whole scene with consummate efficiency – well behind the scenes, mind you, because everyone was made to feel free and happy. Help was available from

With Tommy, Monaco, 1950.

nearby villages most of the time and on the rare occasion when there was none, everyone stepped in and all went smoothly just the same.

The large rooms were beautifully and comfortably furnished with tasteful old and new pieces, enhanced at all times by an abundance of lovely garden flowers. I was strongly reminded of my mother and her talent to create that special mixture of beauty and comfort, without being a slave to fashion and fads. That orthodox sense of 'correct-period-setting', which I find sterile and a matter of vanity and show, deprives a house of its real meaning: a place to live – in comfort. None of that for Kiki. With blithe assurance and inspirational flair she created beauty where old and new could live together, to please the eye, and to give comfort.

The dining table could accommodate at least twenty people, and dinner was always a sparkling affair, not only because of the good home-grown wines, but because everyone was radiating and lively after the day's activities in water and sun.

Conversations ranged from the serious to the downright philosophical, but more often than not, gay and spirited repartee and witty banter ruled the table-round. I was impressed by the young parents' ability to train their offspring in the task of table-help. Part of the holiday-schedule, for them it was almost like a game. Each one of the children had a different task; they would set the table to begin with, and later take away the used settings after every course and deliver them to the kitchen. Here I truly learned to enjoy French cuisine: healthy and hearty, surprisingly simple and delicious, and yet with the occasional sophistication of the gourmet.

The dining room led out onto the large terrace, facing extensive lawns, filled with comfortable garden-furniture. Everyone would enjoy the long late afternoons and evenings there with a cool soft drink, a cocktail, or after-dinner coffee and drinks in relaxed conversation. Occasional guests arrived, relatives or friends, some to stay for the day, enjoying the pool where we all spent a great part of the time.

I particularly enjoyed the walks through the vast park, along the river which cut through the estate. Chestnut trees, age-old, in great numbers, and innumerable melancholy weeping willows. Their image lay still, and only rarely disturbed by a ripple, in a moat-like arm of the river. They form part of a hauntingly beautiful picture, the view from my bedroom window there, indelibly etched in my memory.

One summer, Bea had brought along a young English au-pair girl, Jacky, to help with her three children, a lovely girl with an equally lovely personality. One day, when we were resting in the shade, she confided in me, opening her heart and revealing a profoundly unhappy young woman who had repeatedly tried to commit suicide, held in the tight grip of a deep depression. We went for long walks almost every day, talking and often keeping a companionable silence. She found that she could express her pain, her grief, to me, making her feel freer and clearer in her mind.

I was happy when she gradually began to find her place with the rest of the family. The lively company of the children and the healthy daily routine of play and work did not fail to have a healing effect. She was really beginning to enjoy herself, laughing, teasing the children and playing in happy abandonment. By the end of the summer, I felt she had come a great step forward towards finding and accepting herself, and life. To our profound sorrow she met an accidental death at the age of twenty-three.

In the same summer, Kim, a young Vietnamese man, was hired for the kitchen and to serve at the table. As usual there was a lively conversation flying around the table and suddenly someone opened up the question of homosexuality. Kiki said, 'I can't understand that, nor can I condone it.' I quietly asked her: 'Even if one of your children had this problem?' (Fortunately this was a hypothetical question.) She looked at me in total consternation and after a long while, when everyone was waiting for her answer, she said: 'I could not reject any of my children, come what may!' There followed much debate, much controversy, sharp criticism and harsh judgments, but also questioning voices and open minds, willing to understand.

Kim, the young Vietnamese, had quietly served a second dish, when I voiced my opinion, answering some questions to the best of my knowledge and conscience. I suggested tolerance and forbearance – illustrating the possibility of a genuine disorder in the sexual hormonal system – and the dilemma some such people find themselves in, innocently, in a judgmental society. There was eventually general acceptance although the discussion went on for quite some time.

That evening I heard a knock on my bedroom door. Kim

stood there, tears streaming down his face. He came, he said, because he needed to talk to me. He was a homosexual. It was almost midnight by the time he had finished the harrowing story of his young life. The war, the devastating cruelty he had experienced, the loss of home, parents and relatives, the sexual abuse and persecution. His pain and unhappiness touched me deeply to my innermost being. We had many conversations after that day. I hope that my prayers were answered for his peace of mind.

I enjoyed one or two happy summers in Terraqueuse after I got married to Leslie. But my own wonderful family, my children and their growing offspring – as well as my new family and my lovely new home and husband – but most of all, my ever increasing work as a psychotherapist made it impossible to join Kiki and the happy crowd in Terraqueuse as before.

I was heartbroken when, a few years ago, I received the news of Kiki's death. She had been like a sun, a centre of warmth, for her ever-growing family and circle of friends. I lost a dear friend.

The time I spent in Monaco had been mainly a happy and rewarding time. It had given me a good start on recovery in every way.

Chapter 14

On one of my solitary walks all the way up and out to the Botanical Gardens outside Monte Carlo, I met an English couple that I had occasionally talked to before, and we discovered our mutual love for trees and flowers. After walking through the garden for some time, enjoying the variety and colour of the tropical plants around us, we sat down on a bench. By chance, a friend of theirs came along and joined us and the four of us spent a most enjoyable afternoon together. We arranged to go out to a dinner-dance at the Café de Paris the same evening.

I was quite taken by Mike, who was American. He was gallant, charming and cultured, and very handsome. He declared that it was love at first sight when we danced on the open-air dance-floor in the garden of the Café de Paris. The band was playing seductive melodies and I was taking it all in, like a thirsty soul.

It was a courtship so unusual and charming that it totally swept me off my feet. Before I knew it, we were married in Monaco. I felt loved again. But not for long. Soon after we were married, we decided to accept my parents' invitation to visit them in Giengen on Brenz. It was then, on the road, that my world fell apart once more. A violent rage seemed to shake him, his anger turning against me. He was pulling my hair, trying to push me out of the car, revving up with such ferocious anger that I felt jolted out of my wits. I could not understand what was happening. Who was this man? Just before, we had been chatting about my parents and about his, when he suddenly fell into a rage and lashed out at me, quite out of the blue. My cheek was bleeding and my head was aching. He had pulled out a bunch of my hair and I was reeling as I suddenly realised I had married a man with a very serious problem. He was an alcoholic.

In the middle of nowhere I jumped out of the car to save my life and ran across the fields, utter despair engulfing me. I wandered around, half insane with shock and disappointment, and with disgust at myself. Another mistake! Stumbling about like a drunk, crying silently, muttering angrily, 'When will I ever learn? Why am I so stupid as to fall into another trap?' I slowly calmed down, praying for peace of mind and understanding, and went back to the road where Mike was standing, rather like someone who had received a beating instead of giving it. All the luggage which he had thrown out of the car after me he was putting back onto the roof rack, and we continued our journey to my parents.

Where before I had been full of joy and anticipation to introduce my new husband, now there was a deadening bleakness in my heart and the foretaste of deceit. I did not want to disappoint my parents. Once at their home, Mike behaved as if nothing at all had happened, almost making me believe that it had all been just a dream, a nightmare. We made some lovely tapes of my mother's and father's voices with Mike's rather cumbersome tape recorder – one of the first recording machines – and all in all it was a fairly pleasant visit. My parents were, as usual, generous and welcoming, making him feel at home. He enjoyed himself and there was no sign of his previous behaviour. But my mother, with her keen insight, took me aside one morning and said, 'Are you happy? Are you quite sure he is good for you?' I saw the worry in her eyes and assured her that everything was fine and that I was happy. If only I had had more trust in her love. I can see it now, she was understanding and would have helped to get me out of the trap I was in. If I had confided in my mother, I would have been spared an odyssey of suffering, but also I would have forgone an awesome experience of self-awareness – merciless, yes, but powerfully coercing me to grow up and learn.

We found a flat in Ventimiglia, the little border town between France and Italy, on the Italian side. The sea, the colourful market and the crooked steep little streets of the old town enchanted me and gave lift to my otherwise heavy heart. Marion, at sixteen, budding into a young beauty, enjoyed the enthusiastic admiration of the young Italians. Every night after dinner and two bottles of wine, along with a variety of spirits throughout the day, Mike would start a kind of ritual, a deluge of incessant speech not to be interrupted, gradually turning into ranting and raving about anything in the world. Invariably, it would end in violence. On one occasion he flung the big and very heavy tape-recorder, with those precious tapes of my parents, through the window, down two storeys and out into the middle of the street where it exploded into smithereens. Much later, I discovered that Marion had been sitting outside the door every night, waiting to see if I needed her assistance.

The day came when he attacked and tried to strangle me. She came bursting into the room and pummelled his back so forcefully that he let go. Then the two of us gave him the hiding of his life. Exhausted, we would have liked to go to sleep as he did, but we packed our things, got hold of the little money I had and left. In the train, finally, about ten minutes to departure, there was Mike, walking up and down the platform, shouting and screaming abuse. When the train finally left, Marion and I fell into each other's arms and cried with relief.

Once in Milan, I went to see an old friend. She gave me an introduction to the Director of the British School of Milan who was just then (such luck!) looking for a German teacher. I got the job and could even register Marion for a secretarial course just about to begin. I wrote to Mike, telling him about my intention to divorce him.

This time and space away from Mike gave me the opportunity to do some serious thinking. I wanted to know and understand why I would marry a man with such a problem. Could I not see the signs before? Did I close my eyes to them? It is also true that I knew regrettably little about alcoholism, but did I override my instincts in order to fulfil my fervent wish for a normal family life? Did I just want to please my parents, who so much wanted to see me settled? I also wanted to know why a lovable man like Mike could become an alcoholic; how a person could suddenly change from an even-tempered, charming and affectionate man into a raving maniac, smashing up the house, and almost me too.

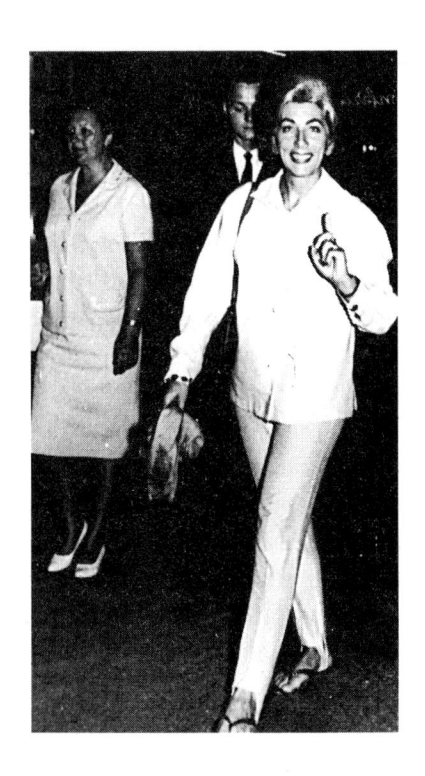

Tour guide in Italy, 1965.

My desire to find an answer to all these questions and to unravel many queries about myself and the world, led me to the University of Milan. It was a long journey of self-discovery and, in fact, more than that – a discovery of the whole human adventure. I did not know until much later that once your partner is married to alcohol, you cannot compete, you haven't a chance. As it turned out in the end, this experience was a blessing in disguise.

I began my studies at Milan University by sitting in on certain lectures on psychology. The books suggested to me by the American lecturer on the subject opened up my eyes to a world of research and greater understanding. Much of what I had lived through took on a new meaning to me. My pain and my reactions, in retrospect, became valuable points of inquiry, some of the pieces of the puzzle falling eventually into place. The law of cause and effect loomed more clearly and beyond that, the importance of compassion, of humanity, in dealing with self or another struggling soul, gave impetus to my further research.

I was able to see clearly that my husband Mike was desperately ill, an illness that had started during his early childhood. He was a man of great potential and talent, unusually intelligent and gifted with an amiable personality. His suffering was submerged, he was tormented by restlessness and pain – inexplicable to him – as if carrying a festering wound, deeply hidden from the world. It seemed he hit out in anger at the one nearest and dearest to him.

Very soon after Marion completed her secretarial course, she was swept off her feet and married Sean, an Englishman living in Milan. Their house was not far from where I lived and we could see each other quite often. It was a life-line for me, as just around that time Mike had suddenly reappeared in my life, assuring and convincing me of his sincere intent to seek help and cure himself of his problem. He even brought a young doctor friend with him to plead his case.

I accepted Mike's goodwill vow to seek help. Through friends of mine, I had heard about a doctor, living in the mountains up on the Italian-Austrian border, who was also a farmer. He would take on Mike in a family situation, where he would have to work on the farm like everyone else. We took the train to the Brenner Pass which was not far from the doctor's farm. A magnificent, stately, old building greeted us and we were given a warm welcome by the doctor, his wife and eight children. It was to be an experiment, where hard work and no alcohol could be beneficial to Mike. He decided then and there to stay and give it a try.

It worked very well. Surrounded by all the children and well-meaning adults, Mike was gradually weaned off the whisky and wine. I visited him once a month, sometimes twice, and was impressed by the warmth of the family life and how well Mike was doing, working quite hard on the farm, like all the others.

I believe it was here where my notion that imagery and relaxation can be very effective in healing emotional problems found its first tentative expression. We had had a long talk, when Mike told me about his inability to relax. I felt that if I could help him to lose his anxieties, he would become more positive in his attitude and his mind and spirit could find rest. I recognised his insecurity and saw suddenly his great need to be loved, to feel safe. My next thought was that I would have to reach out to the child within him. It had been deprived, not of material security, but of a certain maternal care to strengthen his sense of self-worth and his identity. He had told me of his lovely mother, and of his father who had discovered oil and had become one of the big American oil magnates. Their large family of four girls and two boys were brought up in the lap of luxury. However, the father became a workaholic and for his mother, her husband's preoccupation with his work, combined with repeated post-natal depression, drove her into a long period of alcoholism. This had its repercussions on Mike at a sensitive and crucial age. With his mother as role-model, Mike found equal refuge later on in alcohol. He told me how he had so often yearned for her embrace and her love, although he assured me his mother was by nature a very affectionate and gentle woman. Naturally, her affliction alienated her and took her away from him.

'How,' I thought, 'can the gap – the missing out of a sense of warmth and security – be filled so late in life?' I was going to give it a try. All this is an experiment, I told myself. I will play it by ear and see if some of the emotional scars and yearning can be soothed and healed.

Mike was very open to my idea of relaxation. I counted to ten over and over again until he felt the tension ease. I knew nothing about hypnosis then, nor how to go about relaxing someone, but it did work as I just went about it instinctively.

I allowed my fantasies free rein, always having in mind to plant positive, happy and reassuring pictures in his mind. I had become aware of the beneficial effects of positive and constructive thinking to help get one out of a bind, and of the healing power of love. It had become firm knowledge for me without having a logical explanation for it.

I found that Mike was going along with my imagery. I described beautiful, loving angels all around, protecting him. One was the angel of peace, another the angel of self-confidence, then of strength, of courage, of motherly love, of independence, and so on. All of them were giving him of their strength. As a Catholic, he seemed extremely pleased with this picture, and he told me on leaving, 'I have never felt so good and peaceful before. We must do this again.' I repeated the exercise on my next visit and I could see his personality changing. He was happier and more at ease with himself.

The summer came to an end, and unfortunately so did the work on the farm for Mike. The doctor could not afford to keep him on as there was not enough work for him to do. He strongly advised me to find him some work, perhaps doing free-lance English teaching through the British School, to keep him busy. He came back to live with me and I arranged for him to do some private tutoring, which he enjoyed. This was the best time of our marriage, albeit lasting only a few months. I continued with the relaxation for a little while but very soon he thought it was not necessary any more, and concentrated on his pupils.

He had to teach English conversation to two sisters in their home, and that was the beginning of the end. The two girls had been living in a triangle relationship with their uncle, the owner of the flat in which they lived. Both girls were very beautiful and full of charm. Mike got drawn into a sexual relationship with them both, and when I found the three of them together in my bed, that was the last straw. His drinking had begun again and his hostility had become more and more violent every day. This was it. I filed for a divorce, quite relieved to have found a good reason for it.

During all of this time, I had been able to revitalise my scarf design business as a side-line to my job at the British School. Once again it was most successful and I was able to sell to buyers all over the world through Italian fashion trade fairs.

Como is to Italy what Lyon is to France, that is in regard to silk and silk-screen printing. I went to Como and found a factory which would not only sell me the silk and silk-screen print the designs for me, but which would also undertake to have them hand-rolled. One of my bedrooms had become my studio, and I would design the scarves in watercolour, transparent and opaque on paper. The generous size I had used before had proved successful and so I continued with it. Some of the designs were figurative, of flowers or fashion models, and others quite abstract. Each design would be printed in a range of colours and some went to be made into blouses which also sold internationally.

On one of their trips to London, Marion and Sean were passing Harrods in the car when Marion saw some of my scarves spread out in a lovely window display. She shouted, 'Stop, Sean!' and they hurried over to have a good look. I was just as thrilled as they, when they told me about it, to know that my scarves were exhibited in a window of this renowned store.

By the time I had decided to leave Milan and see if I could make my way in the USA, Marion and her husband were living in London. To my dismay, we couldn't meet before I left, so my final telephone bill was rather high!

There has always been something about Marion that at times, as a child, made it quite impossible for me to scold her when she had been naughty. A subtle movement of her mouth, a look in her eyes, reminded me, with a shock, of Klaus, her father. Thank goodness she never knew why I suddenly became lenient, letting her get away with almost anything!

A sudden, transient incident, so small that one might not have noticed it, springs to mind. It was of intense significance to me, though, and I have never forgotten it. Marion was only two. It was on a truck, on our flight from the Russian Army. Hundreds of people, the drift of the dispossessed, not as lucky as we, were lining the dusty road in slow processions, leaving more and more of their burdens behind on the banks. The dust had settled all over us, and I thought we looked like sculptures of stone – clothes, faces, hands, all the same grey. Marion looked at me, wide-eyed, standing before me, quite still. Suddenly a fleetingly brief expression of total knowledge, of a wisdom far beyond her age, coupled with the courage and love of an old sage, touched her face. She climbed up on my lap and gave me the dearest, warmest hug I ever received. Did I put this interpretation into her expression myself? I think not, because on occasion I saw it again and realised I had been seeing something that was there, really a part of her.

Chapter 15

In time I was promoted to Head of the German Department at the British School of Milan, and I also taught and lectured in German and English on a free-lance basis at other language schools in Milan. It may sound a bit contrary, but I found that there is no better way to learn the language of a country than to teach the locals another one. At least this was the most painless way for me to learn Italian.

At the British School I met Dina. She, too, belongs to that small group of people whose friendship I am still enjoying after more than thirty years. A beautiful soprano, she had won a scholarship in her home town in the USA to receive special voice training as an opera singer in Italy. During her studies, Dina was supplementing her income by teaching English at the British School of Milan, and we became good friends. On her departure to her first serious engagement at a German opera house, she presented me with a book, a farewell gift – *The Prophet* by Khalil Gibran. It has since been a constant companion and a wonderful source of enlightenment for me.

When the teaching of languages other than English was discontinued at the British School, I was offered a post at the American Trade Centre which was attached to the American Embassy. Slowly, it seemed, my self-image was mending. I met interesting people within the Centre and without. My language skills suddenly became an asset and I enjoyed the conviviality of the place. My social life was considerably enhanced too. Among my new acquaintances at that time was the Director of La Scala, a charming man. I spent many a wonderful evening at that famous place, often with my son or with friends, listening to the unforgettable voices of Maria Callas and others.

In the summer before I met Mike and left Monte Carlo, my son Tom accepted an invitation from his uncle Fritz, my younger brother. He had emigrated to Melbourne, Australia soon after the war with his wife Karin. Like our father, he quickly established himself and developed a good reputation in the world of export and commerce. They had no children and, as my brother realised my precarious position, he offered to have Tom there and give him a good education at Melbourne Grammar School where, after much effort, he had been able to register him.

When I took Tom to the airport in Frankfurt after a warm farewell from his grandparents, relatives and friends, he whispered, 'Mammi, for heaven's sake, don't cry! Please!' 'OK,' I said, not really knowing if I could handle that order. My sister Kay, who lived in Frankfurt, took us to the airport in her car, and Jost, her son, just a year younger than Tom, came too. With a willpower I don't know how I summoned, I managed to keep the pressure behind my eyes while I embraced him to send him on his way. Behind me, I heard the soft voice of my nephew, saying to his mother, 'Mammi, Tante Ellen is not even crying!' That almost broke the thin line between 'keep smiling' and 'bursting into a flood of tears'. But I did remain outwardly calm, swallowing harder a few times. In the car, later, I allowed my tears to flow freely, telling my young nephew that I had to keep a promise not to cry. 'Oh, Tante Ellen, I think you are a hero!' he said and I gave him a big hug, and was quite willing to accept his praise. I thought so too.

Once Tom had settled in his new environment, I soon received reports from my brother, from his teachers and from Tom himself. Letters were full of good news. Tom's in particular were written wittily and descriptively. He had become quite a sports champion, and at the same time been able to jump a whole class, which he did again the following year. When he reached the age of seventeen, he had already passed his A-levels and was given a university scholarship. Besides that, he was chosen and accepted for the Olympic Games, but he never made any use of either. It seems that over the years homesickness had really set in and eventually became unbearable. I had no idea, as he had never mentioned his longing in his letters. One day I received a long letter from him, telling me all about it, and how in the end, he could not bear it another minute and had decided to go and book his passage back home. When I received the letter, the day and time of his arrival were only five or six days hence, so I hurriedly prepared our guestroom to make it cosy and comfortable for him. All the time my mind was going round in circles: 'What will he think when he realises my marriage is on the verge of breaking up?' At that time I had filed for divorce but was still living with Mike. 'What must his uncle think about his leaving after they had done so much for him?' Well, I did find out about that. They never forgave him, although he did try and explain it to them many times before and after.

On the day of his arrival, Mike and I went to Genoa to pick Tom up at the dock. A tall and slim young man, blond and handsome in a dark blue suit suddenly grabbed me and held me close, whispering into my ear, 'Can you still bark like a dog?'

This time my eyes were brimming over and I could only nod. 'Do it . . . please,' he said. 'Rrraw, Rrraw,' I barked, and he hugged me, lifting me off my feet, hooting with delighted laughter. The barking like a dog had been, and is still, one of my greatest accomplishments, verified by the instantaneous reaction of any dog in the vicinity, invariably going wild and, with me barking back, continuing into quite a débâcle. Mike stood there with us, clearly wondering whether we had gone totally round the bend over the reunion, but soon he couldn't stop himself either and we all laughed till our sides hurt.

Soon enough, Tom realised the state of affairs in our marriage, and I told him about the divorce. His support was wonderful and it almost seemed to me that he had been sent back by a higher power for that very purpose. But why, I thought, should a young man have to give up so much just to assist his mother? That sacrifice seemed wrong to me. But it wasn't. He saved my life. If it hadn't been for him, I would have been killed. After one of his drinking sprees, Mike came home around three o'clock in the morning in a state of total inebriation, shouting and screaming at an unseen adversary. He came storming into my bedroom with a large kitchen knife, stabbing it at me. In spite of being awakened from a deep sleep, I jumped sideways as fast as a flash, and out of bed on the other side. But he cornered me between the bed and the wall. I closed my eyes, paralysed, unable to move. Then I heard Tom's voice as he stepped in between us. 'Drop that knife,' he said, very slowly and with a voice that could strike terror into anyone's heart. His face was white with anger and concern. Mike did, he just dropped the knife, like a child obeying the order. Tom took me by the hand and pulled me into his room.

As usual, the next day Mike was aghast about what had happened, remembering nothing. As there were two of us, and Tom in a deadly mood, he had to believe it this time. After a whole morning of reasoning and pleading, he began to realise that it was too dangerous for all of us for him to stay. He knew, too, that it could easily happen again. His young doctor friend pleaded with me repeatedly not to leave him. 'He loves you, he truly loves you, in spite of his affairs. You have to stay with him, he needs you,' he invariably said. This had brought me back on several occasions after I had left him. As I could not persuade Mike to seek psychological help, I saw no hope any more and felt totally at a loss. I wanted so much to help him too.

On one of those occasions when his violence became too dangerous, I ran away, grabbing my handbag and coat and went to a hotel. I had decided not to go back to him. In my purse was very little money, just enough for one night's stay. Then I remembered my bracelet which I was wearing, several strings of gold chain with a clasp of precious stones. I thought I could always sell that, and went to bed more at peace. The money would coast me over until things could be sorted out.

After I returned from the bathroom in the morning, my bracelet was missing. I was deeply shocked and worried. Then a strange and marvellous thing happened, and that is why I remember this particular incident so well. I sat down near the end of the bed, as if someone had calmly taken me there and sat me down. I relaxed and prayed. Then, again, as if someone was pushing me over gently, my body sank onto the bed and my right arm fell over the end of the bed right into the wastepaper basket standing there. Closing my fingers around something, I had the bracelet in my hand. At first I was utterly dumbstruck, and then I just went into a feast of 'Thank Yous'. My Guardian Angel again?

Pedro, our friend the doctor, once more persuaded me to go back. A book came into my hands: *How to live 365 Days a Year* by Dr Schindler, all about psychosomatic illnesses – addictions, etc. One sentence stood out for me: 'If you are emotionally involved with an addict or neurotic, you cannot directly help him. Help has to come from an outside source, which is emotionally detached.' Suddenly everything clicked into place. He was so right, this Dr Schindler. My search at the University, technical books on psychology and all the manifold discussions with students and teachers had not given me the insight I needed. Now, I felt, I could distance myself without feeling guilty. It was no more my problem.

After our divorce, Mike would still come to see me, even after he had remarried. One day he came to visit me to introduce me to his new wife. That night I had a tragic and prophetic dream. Standing in front of a bathtub, in which a baby was drowning, I was completely paralysed, trying frantically to get at the baby to rescue it, but to no avail. It drowned in front of my eyes. I was devastated. In fact, their marriage was eventually another disaster. I felt the baby of the dream was Mike's new young wife, whom I'd wished I'd been able to warn of the dangers of being married to a man with such an affliction. But I also knew she would not listen to me. I saw symbolically the strength of the drowning man being greater than that of the rescuer. He pulled her down with him. She, too, became an addict and soon after he had committed suicide in his Swiss chalet, she too died.

I had another dream at that time – one that was far more important and from which I have been learning since. I was in a field and I saw three weeds, already deeply rooted in the ground, each different from the other. While I was looking at them, a voice spoke to me, the same voice I had heard once before in another dream. 'Pull them out, one by one.' I did. It was not easy because there were fine little hair-roots tenaciously clinging to the ground.

After I had succeeded in pulling out the first weed, the voice spoke again: 'What you just eliminated was Self-pity.' At this point in the dream, I realised that I was being given a message. Self-Pity? Did I really feel sorry for myself? I did not think so at all. I did not like it though when, on deeper contemplation, I gradually came to the conclusion that, yes, it *was* true! I *did* feel sorry for myself. I had always been thinking, 'Why me? What have I done to deserve this?'

The voice spoke again: 'Self-pity is a heavy chain around your feet. It does not allow you to walk ahead. It is holding you back.'

When I thought about this, it felt as if a stone wall inside me began to crumble. 'Yes,' I told myself. I would try to walk ahead without feeling sorry for myself.

When I began to pull out the next weed, I could already hear the voice saying: 'Blaming Others is the name of this one.' Blaming others? So what? I thought. It wasn't my fault that I was raped as a child. It wasn't my fault that a Hitler came to power, that a brutal war was fought, and I became a victim!

The voice spoke again: 'True, nothing was your fault, not your personal fault. But does it help you to survive, or does blaming others paralyse you on your road forward?' I had to think deeply again. Paralyse is the word, true. It is a totally unconstructive emotion. Come that far in my ponderings, I went on to consider that, yes, I *am* handing over the control of my life to forces outside of me.

By this time I was quite disturbed and concerned about my ability to eliminate those weeds really and truly. What new discovery about myself was awaiting me with the last weed I was now trying to pull out of the earth?

This one seemed to fight back. I kept finding little bits here and there and thought that I just could not get it all out.

'Guilt,' the voice said. Now I was really surprised. I did not feel that I was guilty. In fact I thought others should be guilty about what they had done to me. I could only refute this out of hand. 'I don't feel guilty!'

But then, insistent and clearer than ever, the voice began again: 'Guilt feelings can be justified or totally unjustified, superimposed by negative conditioning. One or the other kind can lie dormant, hidden deep in your subconscious mind. Fear becomes part of it.'

Fear? Was guilt hiding behind fear? Justified or not justified? I was contemplating my young days – happy days, New Zealand, Leipzig. Well, yes, as a child you do a lot of naughty things for which you feel guilty. You get punished and if not, you don't like the feeling your conscience raises and you do better the next time, and all is well again.

Relentlessly, the voice spoke again: 'Did you feel guilty after the rape?' 'Yes, of course,' I said. 'I could not tell anyone about it. I did not understand what was happening to me; my mind seemed to freeze up.'

I was confused. A picture emerged in my mind of the classroom the day after the rape, when the teacher came to my desk and asked me a question. Terrified, unable to speak, I just stared at him. Guilt or fear?

'Stop!' intoned the voice. 'What are you doing, defending yourself? Why? Your assumed guilt, your fear, was totally unjustified. You were innocent. This happened to you as an accident, a tragic, unfortunate occurrence, such as can happen to many an innocent victim.'

An innocent victim? Yes, I was! Why should I feel guilty, albeit subconsciously? Cloaked in a dark cloud of inner restlessness, I never even knew the real culprit.

I began to realise then that I had to work hard, to look deep within myself thoroughly and eliminate the shadows. I now asked the voice, 'But is not a feeling of guilt a good and necessary thing when you have really done something bad?'

'Yes,' was the answer, 'to be acted upon as soon as possible in order to redress the damage, admit the fault and then to start afresh and learn from one's mistake. All is education. We have much to learn from each of our mistakes.'

As I awoke, it was as if I had emerged from a dark, murky pool into clear, clean and fresh air. I had a lot to think about, and even more to do.

Chapter 16

Coming *back to America was like joining up a big circle in my life. The days with Joan had been wonderful, and had now come to an end. The golden wedding party of her parents at the Terrace Restaurant, with the unique view from the roof terrace, was unforgettable and those short days, when I enjoyed Joan's hospitality and her graceful and stimulating personality, would stay with me. Our friendship, warm and enduring, seemed like one of those splendid unexpected gifts. Now it was time for me to continue my nostalgic travels.*

I had decided to take the train to Wyoming, Pennsylvania, home to my friends Dorothy and John. They were expecting me and I was looking forward to being reunited with two very dear people. Fourteen years had passed since I left the United States, and we had kept in touch. Leaning back in my seat, I relaxed and watched some of the old familiar, and some new, landmarks of New York City pass me by, I was inevitably drawn back to memories of when I saw them first in 1966.

When I first arrived in New York, filled with the apprehension of beginning a new life, I was looking forward, open and eager to start. I had rented a furnished apartment in a brownstone house on the west side near Central Park, with a modest sum of money to hold me over for about a year till I could find my feet. Until then I could relax and enjoy all the new impressions flooding into me. I had brought my scarf designs and was going to follow up on an invitation from a Lord & Taylor buyer who had regularly bought my scarves in Milan. She was particularly interested in one design with two roses, freely painted and silkscreen printed on the scarf.

I had been in this apartment less than a month when I went out one evening to see a movie. I came back to find all my possessions burgled – designs, clothes, typewriter, money, even my set of luggage. The police were unable to trace or catch the thieves. All of a sudden, in one night, my life took on a completely different perspective. The implications hit me hard: I would have to find a new apartment and a job, quickly.

I started looking for work, but without a green card, the American work permit, I knew it would be difficult. Finally I found employment as secretary to a designer of plastic furniture in a rather dark and dirty factory district. My employer did not seem concerned about my lack of working papers as long as he could pay me the lowest possible wage, about $100 a week. This, actually, was a king's ransom for me at the time, since I was now quite poor and felt lucky to be able to buy five-dollar dresses in the bargain basement of department stores.

I made frantic efforts to master the typing I had to do. My boss didn't take too kindly to my mistakes, but at least he didn't fire me. He just became quite threatening and unpleasant. My typing did eventually improve, but I was desperate to find another job. I had got to the stage with that job when I dreaded going to work in the morning.

I worked in a dingy little office high up in the building. The warehouse smelled of a mixture of rusty iron, dust, mouse droppings and some indefinable, objectionable odour. The elevator seemed to me to be in immediate danger of falling apart as it clanked laboriously up to the tenth floor. I became more than ever determined to get out of this nightmare. But what could I do? I felt completely at a loss until one day, as I lay on my bed after another dreary day's work, I recalled my father talking about a businessman, a political suspect under Hitler, whom he had helped to escape from Germany just as the War was looming. Father had told me that he had gone to New York. I recollected that my father had received a letter from the man, saying that he had been able to get back on his feet there. The letter was full of warm thanks for the help given by my father and best wishes for our family's fortune. He had said, if ever I can be of help to you, please let me know. But I could not, for the life of me, remember the man's name. I could not ask my father, as he had died two years previously. It was a fairly common name, I knew that, but which one? Anyway, he might have changed it, or he might have moved to California, or anywhere. I lay on my bed, trying to relax and let the name come into my head. To no avail. I tried every day, concentrating, relaxing, hoping to remember the name.

It was quite a surprise when, as I rode up in the elevator one day, thinking about nothing very much, and not looking forward to yet another day in this dirty factory, the name suddenly popped into my head like a bolt of lightning. After that, I rushed into my office and began delving into the pages of the enormous New York telephone directory. But my heart sank. There were pages and pages of them, all of the same name! Still, I thought, there was a chance that my man was one of these, and I would try until I found him, or ran out of names.

It took me weeks of diligently going down the columns of phone numbers, ringing from a phone box in my dinner hour, ringing from the office when the boss was out, and ringing from the phone box near my apartment every evening, getting through hundreds of dimes. Still I persisted and the more I spent, the more determined I was not to give up now.

At last, I was blessed with success. I rang the right number and spoke to a friendly American woman who had married my father's friend not long after he arrived in New York. She knew all about her husband's escape from Germany of course and she immediately invited me to come and see them.

I arrived at a luxurious house in an elegant residential district near New York City. This man had become one of the Vice Presidents of a big international company whose headquarters were in a forty-four storey building in the centre of Manhattan, and had made quite a name for himself. The warmth of their welcome touched me deeply, and later, when I asked for help, I received it.

'I am only too pleased to help you,' he said. 'If it hadn't been for your father, I certainly wouldn't be here now, maybe not even alive.'

I went home that day like a bird on the wing, glowing with happiness and hope.

In the meantime, I had seen a lawyer who had been recommended to me. He asked for my passport and other papers, assuring me that it wouldn't take long to supply me with the necessary immigration papers. I was asked to make monthly payments of fifty dollars. In the meantime, I would hear from him – not to worry. When I went to see him after two months had gone by and I hadn't a word from him, he told me that he hadn't had the time yet to do anything on my behalf, but 'not to worry', he would get on with it now. After a further two months without a sign from him, I went to see him again. I had regularly paid the fifty dollars, but was reluctant to go on with the payments. He seemed quite a different person then. Quite coolly, he said, 'Why don't you marry an American, or go across to Canada to receive a new visitor's visa, and come back here?' It was then I finally realised that I had been taken for a ride. I did get my papers back, but not my money.

This happened about the same time that I had paid down a small amount weekly to an accommodation bureau for an apartment. It was to be vacant and at my disposal within a month, by which time I had paid off their fee. When I arrived on the day I was to move in, with all my bits and pieces, my luggage and all, I found that somebody else had moved in the day before! I am the perfect mug, I thought. There was no way for me to get my money back from this lot, either. However, they were lessons, infuriating, exasperating lessons. They were also a heavy price to pay. It seemed I had to go through a baptism of fire to become New York street-wise. And would I ever?

I remember that night with a dull ache. Having left my things in the care of the lucky tenants, I wandered around the darkening streets of Manhattan, under a black cloud of despair. Looking up at the many illuminated windows, I felt the old familiar sense of loss – an unbearable numbing sense of hopelessness. 'People live in these houses. They all have a home, warm and safe.' Yes, I was feeling sorry for myself, I admitted it, but it did not lift the darkness of my soul. I walked on through the streets like an automaton for hours. Night was falling when I suddenly stumbled and almost fell over a man lying on the sidewalk, halfway into a doorway. 'Was he sleeping off a binge?' I asked myself, 'or was he, perhaps, just another one of those lost souls, depleted of hope and exhausted from trying, unable to fit into the rest of society any more?' A strange, overpowering kinship took hold of me. We were both homeless, I thought. Why don't I just curl up here too, and perhaps die? A memory was stirred up while I was standing there, deep in thought, and suddenly, with all the force of my pain, I began to pray, just as I had done once before in a small garden. It seemed aeons ago when I had prayed with equal ardour for my survival. I had had an immediate answer then. I knew at once that again there would be a solution, an answer to my plea. It felt as if a warm coat of reassurance, infinitely gentle and merciful, was folding around me and telling me, 'Do not worry any more.' Resolutely, I walked on and went to stay with a German friend, Marianne, who willingly gave me temporary shelter. And soon after I found a one-room basement apartment. It was not what I wanted, but it would hold me over till I found the right place. It looked nice. The comfortable bed could be folded up in the morning; it had wall-to-wall carpeting and a french window, leading out into a tiny, neglected garden; and it was nicely furnished. A bar-like counter separated the minute kitchen from the main room and behind the kitchen was the bathroom, looking neat and adequate. I busied myself immediately with making the place more homely, putting up some of my paintings and other familiar things to make it mine.

One evening, after a day's work at the office and a light supper, I was sitting at the table in my studio apartment with Don Mack, my first private pupil for German conversation. A Manhattan language school, where I had registered as a private teacher, had sent him to me. At one point in our conversation, when I looked up through to the kitchen, I saw the most enormous cockroach climbing up the wall behind the fridge. I had never seen anything quite like it. A little scream escaped me, and Don jumped up with me, not knowing why. When he turned round, after looking at my face, and saw the huge black thing crawling up my kitchen wall, he began to laugh, helplessly, with complete abandon. As a New Yorker, born and bred, he'd seen it all before. He knew that a great many houses in New York City were lived in, not only by people, but by much more ancient inhabitants – cockroaches, termites, rats and the like. They lived there to stay. He got hold of my broom, and I of another weapon and a hilarious, wild chase ensued. The cockroach suddenly developed the speed of a UFO. By the time we had caught the innocent invader, our sides were aching from laughter. It was an unusual start to a lesson. Don's good humour and fun-loving nature helped me a lot to get over the rather daunting discovery that the house was infested with cockroaches. I remember thinking that it would have to be sooner than soon that I moved again. But my heart was sinking. 'Is it possible to keep them at bay?' I asked. Don thought that I might be able to control them to a point, but I would no doubt have to accept the company of one or more cockroaches at times. 'They don't bite, you know,' he said with a wicked grin.

Then, one day, Don invited me to his home and I met Joan, his delightful wife, the woman who became a life-time friend, even after their marriage had broken up. When I entered the room that day, she was holding their three-month-old baby in her arms. I stood spellbound for a few seconds, touched by the tenderness of the picture, the still atmosphere, as if time had stopped its race. It was the deep bond between mother and child, the baby's huge dark eyes looking up into his mother's with that infinite trust and complete innocence, that touched a cord deep within me. I made a drawing later, where I tried to capture the intimate, silent communication between mother and child. We had a very pleasant afternoon, but then I had to go home to my cockroaches. I soon realised, however, that the virulent invaders were really small fry compared to the flood of water that poured in from the garden one day. Outside, the heavens had opened and I was totally flooded out. Was the place jinxed? I asked myself.

One day, I was entertaining two lady friends and while we were chatting, having a cup of coffee and cookies, laughing and thoroughly enjoying ourselves, suddenly, for no reason at all, four of my watercolour paintings on the opposite wall came sliding down, silently, one by one. The three of us jumped up, alarmed. 'This is spooky,' Hilda said, and Beth suggested that I check the nails in the wall and the wires on the pictures. I did, and told them they were all intact. By this time, my two visitors were really frightened and in no time at all, they took their leave and were gone. I must admit that I felt quite scared too, but all I could think of doing was to check the nails once more. They were completely fine. I decided to take no more notice, resolutely hung them up again and tried not to think of it any more.

My basement apartment was in close proximity to the boiler room. On two occasions the temperature had risen to about 112°F. I got no end of tummy-bugs and on one occasion I came down with pneumonia. I had to be taken to hospital. Scarcely recovered, back in my apartment, one morning as I was brushing my teeth, looking into the bathroom mirror, I spotted behind me a swarm of termites, a clustering cloud almost barring the bathroom door. They had that very moment come up from out of the bottom of the wooden door-frame to throng higher and higher in their wild wedding-dance. For a moment I was transfixed, dumbstruck! I wondered how I was going to get out of the room. 'Well,' I thought, 'I just won't take any notice of you. I'll have my shower and then we'll see!' When I was done, I splashed as much water as possible in the direction of their crazy dance, enough to give me passage. Without drying myself, I grabbed a towel and dashed out of the bathroom, leaving their ominous goings-on.

That was the last straw. I *had* to find another place to live. Here I was accident-prone, no doubt about it. When I told the termite story to my friend Marianne, she almost had a fit, whooping with laughter. 'These New Yorkers find this sort of thing funny,' I thought, but I had to see the funny side of it myself. I joined in her merriment. The mercies of laughter! When we had eventually calmed down, Marianne came up with a brilliant idea. She remembered having met a German gentleman who owned a house in Jamaica, Queens, and who always seemed to prefer letting his apartments to his compatriots. We went to see him, and luck was on my side. He promised me a very nice place for a price I could afford in his Jamaica apartment building. I had to wait another six weeks in my dungeon, but now that should be bearable. Or was it?

In the meantime, Eric, who had promised to help me, was now happy to be able to reciprocate the assistance he had received from my father. He had put the wheels in motion and a job was available for me. 'A lowly job, to be sure,' he said, 'but it is understood that if you work hard, it will lead to better things,' and it did.

My trials were not over, however, in that peculiarly freakish apartment. The termites were not the last straw by a long shot. More was to come. It started again the day Martin Luther King was murdered. When the doorbell rang, I opened the door to a handsome, buxom woman, who asked me, 'Do you know of anyone who needs a baby-sitter?' I thought for a moment, remembering two of my friends who were looking for just someone like that. I asked her to come in and went to my desk to write down the two addresses. I gave them to her and we spoke a while, mainly commiserating about the tragic death of Martin Luther King whom I greatly admired. Before she rang, I had been on the verge of going shopping. My handbag, ready to go, was on the table near the door. I had turned my back on her for only a few minutes but when I looked into my bag, my wallet was missing – *again*! I thought, 'Will I ever learn to mistrust?' I just could not stop a ghostly smile. 'Wait till I tell Marianne! Nobody will believe me. This seemingly endless, unremitting chain of disasters looks more like a tale from a story-book, a bad one to boot!'

There was, true to a bad story, another straw to follow. It happened just before I could escape from that scary, jinxed place, mocking me and my gullibility. It happened a few months after I started my new job for Eric's international company in the mailroom. I came home to my apartment building one evening. It was just before Christmas. I walked into the lobby, and as I was struggling with a bundle of Christmas cards stuffed into my mail box, a young man stepped up to me and thrust a hard object into my ribs (the blue and green marks lasted for weeks). He demanded my purse which I handed over to him immediately, shocked and frightened, because I could detect the tell-tale look of an addict – a dangerous situation, because in their own state of need and fear, anything can happen. Once he had it, he was away in a flash and out of sight.

On another level of consciousness, I had observed a truck-driver who had watched the whole scene through the window, while parked in front of the building. He looked away and eventually pulled out without any outward reaction at all, which I later found out was a standard example of how many New Yorkers dealt with the everyday muggings and violent acts on their streets. They felt it was foolish to risk their own lives for someone else's money.

My purse had contained all my wages for January, plus a Christmas bonus. Later that week, my purse was returned to me, minus the money, by a woman who, judging by the letterhead, worked for a New York radio station. She kindly wrote that she had found it in the gutter of a neighbouring street. I was pleased to have at least the cherished photographs of Marion and Tom and my granddaughter Fiona returned, but the situation was critical for me, as I was living from pay-cheque to pay-cheque. It was lucky that I had a season ticket for the subway – at least I could go to work.

I felt as though I had been crushed out of existence, stamped out like an ant. When I told my colleague in the mailroom about my disastrous experience the day before, my tears finally began to flow. She was kind and sympathetic, but was poor herself. She helped me in another way, which I didn't realise until later.

While I was sorting out the hundreds of letters, my thoughts kept going round in circles: how was I going to get through the month, how pay my bills, my rent? I was so new in the firm that I did not dare to ask any of my bosses for an advance. While I was carrying the mail up and down the forty-four floors of the company building, I decided to take the bull by the horns and ask the Vice-President, Eric, who had got me the job in the first place, to help me out. When I came back from my tour, however, there was an envelope on my desk, and my colleague told me that John, the head maintenance engineer, had left it there for me. Inside I found a hundred-dollar bill and a note: 'Absolutely no strings attached', signed 'John'. I could not believe it. How could there exist anyone kind enough to give money to a perfect stranger? I realised now that my colleague in the mailing room had mentioned my plight to John.

When I spoke to John and thanked him, I realised that this man was good. Plain good. The goodness shone right through his put-on roughness, lighting up the space around him. I felt as though a ton of bricks had just fallen off my back.

John came up to me one day, and asked me how I was getting over the hold-up. I thought he might be wanting his hundred dollars back, and felt panic-stricken because I had only been able to save up a fraction of what I owed him. To my immense relief, he assured me that I had all the time in the world, if I insisted on paying back the money. He did not really want it back, he said. But he was genuinely concerned about me and how I was coping.

After that, John and I met frequently. I felt his strong personality. His kind and protective manner had inspired in me trust which had eluded me for so long. A friend, companion and protector during the years I spent in New York – John was all that, throughout many of my trials and tribulations. In my own mind, I had called him my knight in shining armour.

He was tall, with a powerful, sturdy physique, and of Lithuanian origin. His face looked as if it had been chiselled out of wood. I knew that he liked to give the impression of being a 'tough guy', but this was far from the truth.

John took me home to Wyoming, Pennsylvania, on many

weekends. There he introduced me to his closest friend, his cousin Dorothy, a woman of great presence, vibrant, generous and fair-minded. We liked each other instantly. Her statuesque and handsome appearance made people turn their heads.

They were happy weekends in Dorothy's and her husband Howie's beautiful home. Their open hospitality and genuine friendliness did me a world of good. I sensed that she well understood my need to feel the warmth of her family and their friendship. When the third of their children got married, I was invited. I had never been to a traditional American wedding before. My curiosity was richly rewarded, when I could be part, from the beginning to the end, of a marvellously colourful, emotionally charged and blissfully happy day. Diana, the bride, looked breathtakingly beautiful and Gus, the bridegroom, couldn't take his eyes off her. At the end of the day, the band was playing and young and old were dancing tirelessly with happy abandon. I had made a drawing, a portrait of Diana, which I gave them as my wedding present, and it stood in the middle of the table amongst the other numerous presents. As I was going on a holiday after the wedding, I had made my apartment available to them as a little stop-over to visit New York before continuing their honeymoon in Barbados.

John and I had a wonderful time that day. As usual, he was attentive and considerate in order to make me feel comfortable in a crowd of people I had never seen before. This gentle giant could not hurt a fly. His kindness and generosity had only one flaw – he seemed unable to accept anything given in return. It put me in a bit of a spot, because I love to give presents too, and to make people happy. In the end, I gave up and allowed myself to enjoy all the good things. I suppose, in the last analysis, I did return in a different way some of the kindness I received.

The time finally arrived to move out of 'hell' and move in to 'heaven'. With John's help, all my things were moved into the new pleasant, spacious and comfortable abode in Jamaica, NY. My luck had changed. I found that a wonderful old tradition in New York was playing into my hands. Every Thursday evening, furniture which was not wanted any more was placed on the sidewalk of the street below, in front of the house. Anyone in need of just that piece, or pieces, could take it away. I found some very practical and beautiful items to begin furnishing my apartment with. And, with the help of John and other friends, it became more liveable all the time.

Not far from my new home, my need for certain pieces of furniture brought me together with a delightful German family. The father had built up a good business in 'old things'. Amongst them I found some splendid antiques – a lovely mahogany desk with leather top, a set of three leather-top tables, and several Chippendale chairs. My search was accompanied by good advice from his wife and great interest in the 'German lady' from the four, white-blonde little girls who looked like organ-pipes and two strapping boys who helped Pa to get the things out of the maze of furniture in the crowded cellar.

Little by little my new abode was becoming a comfortable and pleasant place to come home to, even to enable me to have guests safely. No jinx involved! By a fluke of chance, I won a competition I had entered and won an electric sewing machine. Now I could start making my curtains.

I still had not received any immigration papers until one day a letter came from the Immigration Department saying that I had to leave the country within a month. I was devastated and John, who happened to be with me when I received the bad news, was upset too, but more for me as the floodgates had finally opened. I thought, 'Well, I was wrong. Fate is just teasing me. Something, somehow, just wants to brow-beat me out of existence.' We spoke later when I had calmed down, and with kindness and common sense, John told me that there was really no reason for despair. He suggested I go and see Eric and tell him the whole story. 'He wants to help you, doesn't he?' 'Yes, oh yes,' I reassured myself, and decided to go and see Eric the very next day in his office.

Eric listened with great intensity and said at the end, 'Write out a report of everything that has happened to you since you came here. You will hear from me. Don't worry, things are never as bad as they look.'

In the meantime, Eric arranged a meeting to which a higher official of the Immigration Department was invited. I was asked to recount everything that had happened to me since I had arrived in the USA, which was already quite a saga. The story included the robbery, the shyster lawyer, the fraudulent housing agent, the termite- and cockroach-infested flat, the hold-up and the second robbery.

There was silence after I had finished my report. The official got up and came over to me, saying, 'We are not all as bad as that, you know, Ma'am.' He gave me an encouraging smile and thanked me, shaking my hand. I was amazed and infinitely relieved when eventually my immigration was granted under the New Zealand quota. It did not take too long either to advance from the mailroom. I had been helping out, on occasion, with the French, German and Italian translations and letters. On the strength of that, I was promoted, first to secretary and later on to international secretary, with my salary rising considerably.

After about two years in the job as international secretary, I became restless, as it was not really what I wanted to do ultimately. Every lunch-hour I would make the rounds of the employment agencies in order to try and break out of the vicious circle of secretarial work, the only result being that I was offered jobs with higher salaries. When, on one occasion, I was tempted to accept an extremely well-paid job not entirely office-tied, I finally handed in my resignation. But my boss promptly raised my salary, so I stayed on. Nice as it was, and flattering too, I was still trying to get out of office work.

In my search, one day an agency I had visited before came up with a job which really interested me. The couple who ran the agency were two delightful people who became good friends. They were convinced that they had had a brainwave when they came up with this job for me. It was Director of Volunteers at a New York hospital, with training supplied. The qualifications required seemed to fit what I had to offer. I went to the hospital, and was offered the job. This time there was no way that I could be bribed to stay in my old job, in spite of the fact that I would be going to a lower salary. Eric was sorry to see me go, but understood my desire to work in a field more congenial to my interests. He and his wife Sylvia had been most supportive to me through some very difficult times, and I was immensely grateful to them both. Many times I had enjoyed their hospitality at home: barbecues, lovely dinners and parties at their beautiful house and garden. They were wonderful occasions and were a light relief in my struggle to climb out of adversity.

On the day my immigration papers arrived, John took me out to celebrate the occasion. I had never been to Radio City Music Hall before, and I was quite overwhelmed by its old-time grandeur and splendour. The Hammond organ, the show, with the amazing Rockettes, all created the atmosphere of a true celebration. An exquisite dinner finished off a wonderful day. From then on John and I became much closer and he showed me many of the attractions of the big city: theatre, shows, lovely dinners, concerts and movies. He always found something new and exciting to treat me to.

Chapter 17

Around this time I started painting and drawing again on some of my weekends. Marianne, my German friend, asked me if I would please do a portrait of her. She had seen some charcoal drawings I had done of one of the directors of the company where I worked, and of my friend Eric, the Vice-President. She thought that the likeness I achieved was remarkable and asked if I could do the same for her in watercolour. 'It will be a challenge for me,' I said. 'I'd like to try, but I've never done a portrait in watercolour before.' She sat for me a few times. It was a struggle, but in the end I succeeded. Marianne was over the moon.

I was thrilled that a new door had opened for me and started a portrait of her little dachshund, called Winzig, meaning 'tiny'. When I had finished the painting, everyone couldn't help smiling, looking at it. I had captured the slightly naughty, yet guilty expression in his eyes and posture.

One day, Marianne had guests at the house and one of them was the owner of a Manhattan gallery. She looked at the two paintings which Marianne

Fiona aged 4. Drawing in charcoal and sepia.

Marion and Fiona, 1968.

had framed to their advantage and given prominent space on the wall of her elegant home.

'Who did these paintings?' she asked.

'A friend of mine, she did them quite recently.'

'I'd like to have her in one of my exhibitions,' she continued. 'Tell her to give me a ring.'

When I called her, she asked me how many paintings I would have available for an exhibition. When I told her 'none', she asked if I could have twenty paintings ready for an exhibition in five months. With some trepidation, I told her I would try.

I was surprised, happy and excited – now I had even more motivation to paint. I went to the zoo to draw some animals, to the park to paint flowers and children, and did some landscapes from memory and imagination. By the time the opening came around I had eighteen paintings – more than I had hoped to produce.

I invited my children with their families from London and Milan to come over for the opening. Two weeks before, I had planned a holiday for us all in Provincetown where I had been able to rent a cottage. Tom had no difficulty in driving the big station wagon I had rented and which could hold us all: Marion and her four-year-old daughter Fiona, Tom and his wife Sylvana, and me. It was a jolly trip and our holiday at the seaside in Cape Cod can only be described as marvellous. Exploring the Cape, swimming in the ocean, and eating the most delicious lobster salad sandwiches, sold near the beach, the likes of which I have never been able to encounter again.

Next door to our cottage lived a young man, a lobster fisherman, with whom we all became very friendly. On one occasion, he brought us an enormous lobster and prepared it for us, and we all enjoyed it together on the big table in front of the cottage, along with all kinds of other good food. Tom had seen to the right kind of wine to go with everything, and it turned out to be a wonderfully happy evening, stretching into the wee hours. In the course of the evening, after Fiona had truly tucked in with enthusiasm, amusing us all with her newly-acquired American accent, she fell asleep right there on the bench. Her mother put her to bed, this time without one of the obligatory bedtime stories. The sun and the sea, the freedom and the togetherness, made it one of those unforgettable holidays of a lifetime.

Soon after our return, the exhibition opened. We were all beautifully tanned, sun- and sea-refreshed and wind-blown. It was my very first exhibition and I was a bit jittery. My expectations swung from fear of total disaster to visions of glory and

My exhibition in New York, 1969.

recognition, only more of the former. The gallery was beautifully decorated with lovely tropical flowers, and their heady fragrance filled the rooms. Snacks and wine were offered, and the place filled quickly. There were three other painters exhibiting – one a Haitian naive painter and two others of completely different styles. I thought it was a very good combination.

I kept in the background to watch the development from a safe distance. I could not see anyone taking a particular interest in my paintings. My heart sank. 'A flop!' I thought and walked away to entertain some of my friends. John and Dorothy had been there from the start and Marianne arrived soon after. When I came around the next time, I noticed a little red spot on two of my paintings. My morale lifted. Then I saw Imre, an old friend, who complimented me by buying a watercolour I had done in Cape Cod. 'I had no idea that you were a painter too,' he told me.

I felt content and happy. Even if I didn't sell another picture, I thought, it must be considered a success for a first exhibition and I told myself that I mustn't expect the moon. Tom came up to me with John and Marion and whispered in my ear, 'A lady just bought three of your pictures.' I was electrified and began to feel the warm glow of success.

It was nice to see Imre again. It had been so long. I had met him soon after my arrival in this city. We were both invited to the same party. My invitation had come from a man whom I had met a couple of years earlier at the US Trade Centre in Milan but, when I received it, I couldn't put a face to his name. I called him up later and asked, 'How did you know where to send the invitation?' By a lucky chance,' he said, 'a friend of mine works in the same company as you.' I now somehow began vaguely to remember him – a transitory meeting at the same table in a restaurant at the Centre, when he had started a conversation and later asked me out to dinner. I declined as I was otherwise engaged. This brief encounter now clearly emerged in my mind and I accepted his invitation with thanks.

'I hoped you'd accept – a second refusal would have been too bad, you know. I have an acquaintance who has agreed to be your escort. He will pick you up on the evening.' That was Imre.

What I experienced at that party in a beautiful home on Fifth Avenue gave me, well . . . pause for thought! There was certainly an amusing aspect to it, but also a significant and timely warning.

Imre was a stockbroker on Wall Street. He called for me at the appointed time and my first impression was: 'Thank Heaven, a gentleman!' Quite unlike other men I had met in New York who might call me up after I had spoken to them perhaps only once with the suggestion, 'How about it?' 'How about what?' I would reply naively at first, until I learned to regard the phrase – a going expression – more realistically.

As I can see it now, it was that party and what went on there that threw some light on the pitfalls of the New York 'High Life', particularly for someone like me, alone and penniless, who had to work hard to make ends meet, but who mainly needed to regain her equilibrium.

Imre's gallant ways reminded me of Klaus and my father. It was quite a relief. The house was one of those fabulous old, imposing buildings on Fifth Avenue. The door opened, and there, exquisitely curvaceous and very beautiful, stood a lady, glamorous jewellery around her neck, wrist and ankles, her hair delicately adorned with glittering gems – stark naked, except for a sheer veil of gossamer silk draped around her shoulders, which she kept arranging with elegant movements of her lovely hands, glowing jewels on every finger.

She welcomed us and charmingly invited us to come in. She led us to our host, after taking our coats, and then proceeded to introduce us to the other guests with the utmost formality. Imre and I exchanged furtive looks and I realised that my escort fortunately had a delightful sense of humour. He grinned and winked at me, and I murmured out of the corner of my mouth, 'Keep your eyes off her, or else!' Our banter went to and fro and gradually we made the rounds, circling amongst the elegant crowd, dressed in all the latest fashion. We were enjoying the champagne and the delicious canapés being served, chatting a bit here, a bit there. Slowly I was beginning to get rather bored, determined however to make the best of it.

Suddenly we realised, with scarcely suppressed giggles, that we were both doing the same thing: watching the ladies, who looked impressive in super-elegant haute-couture garments, watching, in turn, their husbands stealthily out of the corner of their eyes. The husbands, equally impeccably attired in black evening dress, were risking glimpses every now and then to feast their eyes on the beautiful figure of the 'hostess'.

The food was excellent, the champagne splendid, and in spite of the fatuous conversation with a couple who enthusiastically extolled the benefits of a hot bath with a cold shower afterwards, we were having fun. Our conversation was interrupted by our host who whisked me away to introduce me to a gentleman who wanted to meet me. He was the owner of a famous fashion house and, as I am very interested in fashion, and had been in business designing scarves myself, we had something to talk about. I began to weary, though, listening to his interminable lecture on the current state of fashion, and my thoughts were drifting until I heard the by now well known and dreaded phrase, 'How about it?' filter through to my ears. This immediately jerked me out of my reverie and I looked around for Imre. He had been keeping a wary eye on me and must have sensed my dilemma. He came over, asking me if I'd like to go and have a look at some of the wonderful Impressionist paintings which were displayed on the walls of the house. I was greatly relieved to have a reason to excuse myself, and we wandered through the other main rooms. I was enchanted by the Monets, Renoirs and even Van Gogh paintings our host had acquired with his vast fortune and with a keen eye, over a lifetime.

The headache I had been fighting off all day began to come on again with a vengeance. The aspirins I had taken in the afternoon had worn off. I told Imre how I felt and asked if he would mind taking me home. 'Of course not,' he said. 'Let's go,' and I detected a hint of relief in his voice. We exchanged an understanding smile, and I assured him that my headache, convenient as it might be, was unfortunately real. He went to see our host to say goodbye, but he would not hear of it. He suggested instead that I should lie down on his bed for a while and then gave me some more pain-killers.

I lay on the bed in the most elegant bedroom I had ever seen. Closing my eyes, I rested deeply for a while and was beginning to feel well enough to contemplate joining the others, when the fashion-house tycoon came into the bedroom, sat down on the side of the bed and, before I could get out, had started making sexual overtures. It took a fair bit of firm conversation before I could convince him that I was not out for a quick 'lay', and that I genuinely had a headache. Besides, I told him, I really didn't fancy him. Then I made a sharp exit.

Imre seemed relieved to see me again, and when I told him about my doubtful conquest, he said, 'Well, Ellen, that's nothing. Just look along the corridor and see what's happening there.'

I went with him and noticed several people looking through holes and keyholes in the doors, watching. I suddenly felt incredibly stupid. I had been totally misunderstood by the wretched man. He had probably been quite used to ladies disappearing into bedrooms, feigning headaches, expecting their further entertainment.

We quietly tiptoed to where our coats were and slipped out of the place with a sigh of relief. I asked Imre, once we were outside, how he came to be invited to this party. 'Oh, I'm only his broker, and I suppose he was trying to give me a treat. Well, he gave us both a treat, only not the way he anticipated.'

I cannot imagine a merrier end to the strange evening on Fifth Avenue than the spectacle of us both skipping along the deserted streets singing silly songs. We went for a cup of coffee in a tiny café with a feeling of deliverance. In the course of our conversation, I mentioned that I was simply not ready or willing for any close relationship. He looked at me thoughtfully and said, 'That's fine with me. I lost my wife four months ago. I thought I would never get over it, but you made me laugh again for the first time. Thank you. One day I will get over it completely, I'm sure.'

We saw each other on and off over the years, to share a friendly dinner and recount experiences of living in New York. Thinking of him always raises a smile; he was a nice man.

It was not long after that party that I met John, and what a relief that was. The 'party people' had left a bad taste – a quicksand vision – in my memory. I was glad to be on safe ground with him, able to be myself and learn to trust again.

The day after the opening of the exhibition Marion discovered a small notice in the newspaper, reporting on the event. She read out: 'Ellen von Einem's watercolours of children and flowers are superb.' Just one little sentence, but it gave me a great feeling of confidence.

After the opening, the exhibition went on for another week. All but two of my paintings were sold. In the meantime, the departure of my family crept up. It was hard to see them off, quite a few tears were shed. Everyone was going back to their own lives again after a brief period of warm and happy togetherness. I thought it is that very thing – that we all have our own lives to live – that makes the meetings so special and precious.

As I relived those days in my mind, I must have drifted off to sleep, and was awoken suddenly as the train pulled noisily into a station which the conductor announced on the loudspeaker. I had been lost to the world in my reminiscences, back in New York, remembering vividly those years of struggle, fun and success. It seemed important that I should return here now, at this stage of my life, when so much had settled and the lessons so painfully learned had blossomed into a new awareness.

There were a few people left in the compartment now and the silence, almost enhanced by the rhythmic drumming of the train wheels over the sleepers, was only broken by the occasional sound of hushed voices from behind me. 'Only another hour,' I thought, looking at my wristwatch. 'Dorothy and John will be waiting for me at the station.' I was looking forward so much to their company and seeing the family again. I got all my things together, ready for my arrival, and then sat back down and gazed out of the window. America – 'land of opportunity'. Certainly, many opportunities had come my way in which to learn and grow. Now I felt more appreciative of all those things that really count, and had a readiness to enjoy life with all its sorrow and joy.

When I found myself wrapped again in one of Dorothy's and John's long bearhugs, I felt home again. Their joy on seeing me was matched only by my own. Our friendship had withstood time and distance, making all the years in between melt away.

Chapter 18

THE DAY *I arrived, Dorothy and I had talked into the night in the den, a wonderfully cosy room with enormous, comfortable chairs. Earlier on, Howie, Dorothy's husband, had come back from a fishing trip on the Susquehanna river, arriving almost at the same time as Dolores, their youngest daughter, and her boyfriend Peter. Howie, a kind man, thoughtful and usually quiet, spread his catch on the kitchen table with an expression of total delight and pride on his face. 'There, folks,' he said, 'dinner for a king!' Trout of impressive sizes and colour and all sorts of other river fish, big and small, were slithering about on the table. We were all full of praise. His face lit up as he told us with a wide grin and an infectious chuckle how he had coaxed and finally caught the biggest of them all. Then he went on to tell us about his near dip in the river when his boat almost capsized. His dry and self-deprecating humour had us all helpless with laughter, and the leg-pulling and teasing kept us all in a happy mood.*

By that time we had settled down in the den. I remembered, all of a sudden, another fun time I had had with Dorothy. I could not resist a smile at the memory and decided to contribute to the merriment.

'Do you remember your visit to our former home in Shropshire, Dorothy?'

'Of course I do, Ellen.'

'Do you remember the field in front of the kitchen window?'

'Oh, no! Ellen,' Dorothy moaned in mock indignation. 'You're not going to tell them that, are you?'

'Why not?' I said. 'You were the object of great ardour and admiration.' I continued undaunted: 'We had a splendid view over a large field from our kitchen window and Dorothy had discovered some bushes full of sloe berries when she had been out on one of her strolls across the fields. She decided that we must have some to make sloe gin with and decided to pick some for us. A sizeable flock of sheep was grazing contentedly on the fresh grass. Resolutely Dorothy walked right through them to the hedgerow beyond where the sloes were to be found. "It's a nice thing to have in the house, you know," she had said, "to offer to your guests." Leslie and I watched her from the kitchen window as she was filling the basket with sloes. One of the sheep seemed to be particularly friendly and unafraid. It came up to her and Dorothy, animal-lover that she is, put her hand on its head, murmuring endearing words. The sheep liked it – in fact, it liked it too much. It became quite persistent in its attentions until it dawned on Dorothy, and also on us, watching from the window with growing concern, that this was in fact a ram. He had become quite excited and dangerous now, and Dorothy suddenly took to her heels and fled. I've never seen anyone fly across a field with such speed, the ram right after her like the leaping devil. He felt betrayed, surely. Dorothy finally outmanoeuvred him by a few paces and took the low wall with a superb jump that could have put any athlete to shame, landing on the other side with a visible sigh of relief. When she saw our grinning faces at the window, she almost collapsed in laughter and came running round to the back door of the kitchen where all three of us laughed till we cried. Dorothy's sense of escape and the picture of the two racing across the field kept us laughing for days.'

In the den my story had started up the jokes and the teasing again and I thought a bit ruefully, Poor Dorothy will never hear the end of this. After everyone had gone to bed, Dorothy and I sat quietly and enjoyed the peace, listening to the wind which had *suddenly come up. It was moaning and wailing around the house, a plaintive, lonely sound as if from a lost soul. For a while we talked about old times, enjoying our togetherness and the peace, enhanced by the rattling of the shutters, the wind demanding entrance into our little sanctuary. We spoke about the time when I lived in New York and worked at the hospital. She had met a few of my colleagues and friends at the odd social gathering there. She loved to come down to New York once in a while, combining shopping with visits to friends and relatives.*

'Did you know that Steve Adams died last week?' Dorothy suddenly asked me.

'Oh,' was all I could say. I was shocked and sad. 'The epitome of good humour, good sense, and a heart of gold,' I said after a while, 'What a sad loss for his family, and us.' He had been a good friend to the three of us, Dorothy, John and me, for a long time and now he was gone – for us, anyway. My thoughts tried to visualise his kind and humorous face and I was lost in the memory for a moment, wondering where he would be now.

Dorothy had disappeared into the kitchen, returning with two colourful mugs, filled with steaming hot chocolate, my favourite nightcap. 'That will cheer you up a bit before you go to bed,' she said, and put the mug on the little table in front of me.

Earlier she had told me of her plans to visit Germany, beginning her journey in Munich, and travelling north towards Hamburg. After that she would like to come and see us in our new home, overlooking the gentle hills of the Welsh border country which she had not yet seen.

'We've run out of sloe gin, Dorothy,' I said, 'and unfortunately there are no sheep in close vicinity now. I hope you're not disappointed!' I teased.

With the tiniest smile, she said, 'The words "sloe gin" and "sheep" don't belong to my vocabulary any more. So, you see, I have no idea what you are talking about!' Her tiny smile now turned wise and warm when she hugged me and gave me a peck on my cheek. 'It was so much fun to wander around in the fields and in your beautiful, unspoiled little town on the Welsh border. It was a wonderful visit! It seems like only yesterday that we saw each other last. Sweet dreams, Earth Mother. Good night.'

She had always called me Earth Mother from the beginning, and I still don't know why, because I thought that the name was far more appropriate for her — the vital centre of a big and loving family. She radiated life and joy, an inspiration to them all.

Once in my comfortable bed, I thought that I would drop off in no time at all into a deep sleep, but no such thing. Instead I lay there peacefully, letting my thoughts wander where they wanted to go. The news of Steve's death had been bad news, and my thoughts went to the Hospital and my work there. My work as a Director of Volunteers and later of Public Relations had become more interesting as time went on. I got involved with many young people and also those older, some with serious problems like drug-addiction and certain life-threatening situations. Some of my colleagues called the addicts 'No-hopers', people whose hopes had been replaced by regular sorties into oblivion at the end of a needle.

One of my jobs there concerned overseeing the programme of voluntary help which was operating in the Hospital in all the various aspects of functioning. There were volunteers, young and old alike, in the administrative offices and in the different departments like Nursing, Haematology and Bacteriology, and in Social Services, etc. My job was to recruit volunteers, a task which took me into schools and other groups and institutions where I was asked to give talks. There was always great need for helping hands and great willingness from all these sources to help and to be trained for a certain job in the different departments. Training was another of my responsibilities.

In my hospital office, c.1972.

As Director of Public Relations, I wrote articles and reports for several newspapers in order to raise money for the Hospital. I also gave talks to clubs like the Kiwanis, the Lions and the Rotary to give the community an idea of the struggle in a voluntary-aided hospital to survive without subsidy. In the modern world of ever new technological inventions, it became near impossible to keep pace with the increasing expenses.

Dr Frost was in charge of a programme for drug addicts. He worked with methadone, a drug to replace the original culprit with slow withdrawal. His Outpatients Clinic brought in a lot of young people. It broke my heart to see their faces, often void and desolate. We had lunch together one day in the cafeteria and he looked a bit under the weather. I asked him what the matter was.

'Oh, I just don't seem to get very far with these drugs,' he said. 'It seems to me that this problem goes much deeper. These people have a need that cannot altogether be cured or filled with medication. Their need goes deeper and has to do with something missing in their lives.'

'Love, you mean,' I said.

'Precisely, Ellen. You hit the nail on the head.'

He was pleased to vent his feelings about the observations he had made.

'These people have no self-esteem. They think so little of themselves and of others. It is heartbreaking. Some I can send to Release, which is an excellent rehabilitation centre – a wonderful place for these kids, or anyone else coming off their devastating habit. But there should be hundreds of these places, or even thousands. The need is cruelly urgent. But there's just never enough money. Yet, every little bit one can do *is* important. And I was wondering, Ellen, if you might perhaps be able to do a bit of group counselling?' Not waiting for my answer, he continued, 'I happen to have a son in our district school who was present at one of your talks. You seem to have a very special way of relating to young people. Do you think you could give them a bit of your time?'

I was surprised and warmed by his compassion and promised to give it a try.

'I will see if I can get a little group together. I'll have to feel my way, Don. You see, I have never done anything like this before, and it might not work.'

He smiled warmly and said, 'I have total confidence in you, Ellen. I'm sure you'll be able to give them something worthwhile to think about and help them to find their self-esteem, perhaps for the first time. And,' he continued, 'if you find you can't do it, then you can always say that you tried.'

I told him that I had found that many of my young volunteers, when they arrived, were sometimes a rather unruly and disoriented lot. However, they soon changed enormously for the better when they began doing valuable work, appreciated by the recipients of their help. Their morale was lifted and I could almost watch the transformation from day to day. Their demeanour expressed, unknown to them, a certain pride and self-assurance and an endearing sincerity. They were respected. Was there a chance for some of the addicts?

At this point my thoughts wandered back to a curious experience I had had in the New York subway, the underground train. It was a dreary, rainy day and it had been a hectic day too, for me. I had given three different talks in three different parts of the city and had to stay late in my office to catch up with my current work. In the subway train I dropped onto a seat, dead-tired and hungry. Suddenly a gang of girls came storming into our compartment, the last in the train, knives and sticks in their hands, screaming all kinds of abuse at the tops of their voices. Lately the papers had been full of this new wave of crime fashion. Only the night before, a gang had violently marauded and attacked passengers while they stormed through the aisles of the subway train with devastating, and in one case fatal, consequences.

Momentarily the girls stood there in threatening posture, brandishing their weapons. I looked up at them, half asleep, yet aware of danger. In some way, though, I could not be frightened. I think I was just too tired. I realised, however, that the faces of some passengers looked totally terrified. One of the girls, obviously the gang leader, caught my gaze and came striding up to me, shouting, 'Don't you stare at me with those blue eyes, you white bitch!' Very quietly, and quite undisturbed, or so it must have seemed to the other passengers, I beckoned to her to bend down. She did, obviously curious as to what this woman had to say. I whispered into her ear, 'What would your mother say if she could see you now?' The effect of my words, gently spoken, had the most extraordinary impact. First she called her friends over and screamed, 'What would my mother think?' Then there was absolute silence for a moment. She studied my face and suddenly knelt down at my side, forcefully pulling up her sleeve to show me her arm. It was unblemished. 'No needlework, see?' she said, with an expression of anxious entreaty. 'See? Nothing! We're only high on a few beers, nothing else.' Had she perhaps thought that I knew her mother? At any rate, I thanked my guardian angel for the little brainwave. To this day the total reversal of her behaviour and that of the other girls remains a remarkable experience. I still think it was touch and go.

The other girls came crowding around me to show me their arms. Their close proximity to my nose, however, told me that their 'few' beers must have amounted to rather a heavy binge. The rest of the passengers had been watching these strange goings-on with more than a little interest, looking at me perhaps as some kind of witch-doctor. The gang-leader, whose name, I discovered, was Paula, came to sit next to me and we began to talk. I spoke of my work with the volunteers and how much everyone enjoyed it. Soon my card, with my name and hospital address, went the rounds and two or three of them promised to come by at the hospital next day.

After I left the train, I thought I would never see them again. I was sure they were too much under the influence to remember a thing. But I was wrong. The next day, Paula and one of her friends came to my office. I gave them all the information on training, regulations and the time-table, etc., and with unexpected enthusiasm, they accepted their pink, candy-striped volunteer uniforms and started their training the following day. To my greatest joy, one of them later turned out to be a marvellous volunteer, dedicated, compassionate and efficient. She was one of the best in my terminal cancer programme, as in this group I could use only certain people who had shown a sincere desire to help and who were at the same time intelligent enough to realise the patients' mental and spiritual, as well as their practical, needs.

Eventually, I had put together a group of volunteers, including my two subway girls and several of Dan's addiction wards. Quite a mixture, I thought, which might prove beneficial to everyone. Every Friday we got together in my apartment. It was an eye-opener to me to listen to the voices and attitudes of these boys and girls when they came out with sometimes profound thoughts and inspired insights. The discussions, often heated but always in the end down to earth, practical and constructive, revealed the desperate dilemma they were in and the admirable courage of these young people to fight for a place in today's materialistic world of greed and loneliness, exposed to seemingly insurmountable odds. They came from broken marriages or drunken parents, and were often exposed to incredible cruelty. It seemed to me that nowhere could I find that they had enjoyed real love and care. They were ships without a rudder in a sea of cold indifference.

Sometimes I had to hold back the urge to weep. It was the longing in every one of these young people for something they could not name, something beyond their reach, a desperate search, that moved me. There were moments of poignant revelations when one or other of the group revealed their inner confusion and pain. Everyone's heart was touched. An immediate rally around the unhappy one ensued, showing compassion, tenderness and gentle nurturing and care, often with a recognition of their own, identical dilemma.

Their need to feel that they counted for something was appallingly evident. I wanted to find ways to release their insecurities, their fears and need to find oblivion. I also wanted to give them a glimpse of a wider world, a world that included the spirit, a world that included love.

It was here that the idea of deep relaxation struck me again. It had worked, if only temporarily, for my husband Mike. Would it work for them? I did not want it to be hypnosis although, in good hands, that too can be a wonderfully liberating tool to heal the mind. But I wanted it to be more like a guided meditation, or like a prayer.

When I suggested to them that we try this, I was happy and made confident to see and hear that my young friends felt totally safe and reassured of my love and desire to help. Their trust was implicit and they went along enthusiastically into an experiment which, for me and them, meant covering new ground. My desire and idea was to unburden their minds, to unload the anger, frustration, deep hurt and anxieties – albeit only for a while. With repetition, however, I hoped it would have lasting effect. Could their negative feelings and thoughts be re-programmed? Deep inside me I knew it could be done. Had I not done it myself? What I needed was trust, trust in my own ability to show them new horizons, a new way of looking at themselves and the world. In short, to open up their understanding that we have to nurture the spiritual part of ourselves as well as the mental and physical. 'We train and exercise our bodies – ideally, anyway,' I said. 'What about training and exercising the spirit? Isn't the spirit part of our make-up?'

'I suppose so,' said Bruno, a lively and intelligent boy of seventeen. 'But what part of us is the spirit? Do we have to go to church and pray, or do good things all the time, whether we want to or not?'

Everybody was waiting for my answer, a notion of light rebellion in the air.

'I think,' I said after a pause, 'that every one of us has a soul, a spirit, and that we have to give it care, and accept the fact that it is present in us. Spirit has more to do with love than anything else, with *real* love, not all those things that go under the guise of love like dependency, martyrdom, need, eroticism and possessiveness. There are many emotional expressions hiding behind the mask of love. It is a much misused word. Real love has no strings attached. When you love, you want what's best for the one you love.'

Paul said, 'I'd have to be a saint to be able to love, then. When I love something, I want to have it, to possess it!'

Anne, one of the subway girls, said, 'Maybe love means when you always want to do something for someone and you don't really care if you get anything in return. What I think you feel, Paul, is more liking, wanting and needing. Perhaps you haven't come across real love.'

I quickly intervened: 'There is nothing wrong with wanting, liking and needing. It's just not love, as Anne says. It has to do with fulfilment and gratification of the ego. It can become destructive, if pursued at all costs, but in itself, if it does not infringe on other people's rights, it is quite okay and somehow the privilege of youth.'

I continued, feeling their intense interest. 'What we need to recognise is that we are not alone. There is always help available from a higher source, a benevolent, not punishing, source which reveals itself to us in many mysterious ways if we let it. We *do* receive guidance and courage. Maybe we can achieve a closer understanding of all this through deep relaxation. Then we can allow ourselves to rest from all our struggles and open up our creative channels, allowing the life-force or whatever you want to call it to flow. I think of this energy as a current, as if we had plugged into the mains, as it were.'

As we talked, I noticed suddenly that their eyes were bright and shining with a fire lit from within. A sudden connection had been made, like the start from a jump-lead, and a new energy was buzzing around.

The first session of deep relaxation was a marvellous success. Their faces were relaxed after I had finished, with an expression of inner calm, and we parted that day, feeling at peace with the world. Everyone was looking forward to the next meeting. I had eventually developed a method to relax everyone easily, suggesting they inhaled peace and love, strength and understanding with every breath they took in, and breathed out to release all the pain and anger; in short, all the negative thoughts and feelings. I then reminded everyone of their hidden powers and the real inner strength lying dormant within them. In my words to them, it was my aim to bring about a reversal of their negative emotional world through encouragement towards a positive view of themselves, their life and future, to open doors from an entrapped existence, changing the coat of the victim into that of a winner.

We met fairly regularly for well over a year, the sessions of deep relaxation alternating with musical contributions – guitar playing, singing and poetry, mostly created by my young friends. I was astounded and delighted with the talent that revealed itself, and the fact, which I had suspected, that their search for a deeper involvement with life had now found an outlet and a new expression. The former addicts had been coasting along with the others, inspired and encouraged until their own will for survival had been strengthened to the point where they were able to quit. The enthusiasm, the great compassion and kindness amongst them, whether black, oriental or white, was ever and again to me a source of wonderment.

My prayers were full of thanks. It had been a bonus in my job that I was allowed to give away scholarships to those I considered eligible. They were made available to me from different charitable groups. Some of my young friends were eminently eligible and I could pass on to them the promise for a better future. When I was suddenly taken ill with a heart attack, I was somewhat relieved to think that those young people had something solid on which to build their futures, something no one could ever take away from them – a sense of their true selves.

The heart attack, coming out of the blue as it did, was the

culmination of a complex and unresolved conflict in another part of my life. It shook me into facing an awful truth, as so many of my experiences had in the past.

A newly-installed employee, in charge of Administration, had taken a strong dislike to me. I could not for the life of me understand why he was trying to provoke me continually with absurd accusations. I cannot say that I took his blatant insults lying down. I found out that he was divorcing his German wife, that he hated Germans, and that he had his eye on my position for his girlfriend. That, at least, explained things, but did not help me to overcome my feelings of anger and frustration.

The building, housing my beautiful and roomy offices, had to be torn down. A huge building project was under way to enlarge the capacity of the hospital and modernise it. In the meantime, some department heads, whose offices were also in my building, were given temporary space elsewhere. We had no choice in this. But all of those who had to be moved were fairly satisfied with the substitute rooms made available to them. Bar me.

To my shock and surprise, and everyone else's, I was given a small room, a former storeroom, next to the kitchen. This was to be, and became, my office, although there was space available, much healthier and quite adequate for my staff of three and me, elsewhere. I had a wonderfully efficient secretary, Anna, a young woman with a lovely face and figure, who sadly had a handicap: one of her legs was thinner and shorter than the other, owing to severe polio as a child. She and my faithful assistant Joe, both of Italian descent, were of great value in my work. One could say we were like-minded. They were of enormous support throughout. Then there was LeRoy, handsome, reliable, efficient and brilliant. My young Head of Volunteers could detect those young volunteers who thought I was a bleeding-heart liberal who would lean over backwards to help them because of their colour. One day, I heard him say to a group who had behaved rather badly, 'Forget about your colour. You don't get away with this any more than anyone else here. Ellen doesn't see the colour of your skin, she only sees your inside. She treats everyone alike.'

We tried to bear the crowded situation with fortitude and humour. The temperature was a regular 95°F and rose at times to over 100°F. I found a space for my secretary in another office eventually, and the others had an ingenious way of finding work outside the office most of the time. The cockroaches had a good time chasing each other and taking absolutely no notice of any deterrent efforts on our part. Of course, I had by now become a New Yorker in a fashion and cockroaches did little to unsettle me, but that doesn't mean that I didn't dislike them heartily.

I tried to fight my anger and the frustration which kept rising in me, something I can only describe as hatred for the man who continued to dog me. My mind was going round in circles. How was I going to get out of this unbearable situation without letting him win? There seemed to be no exit.

I finally convinced myself that I just had to grin and bear it and forget about the man. Just then I came down with a heart attack. Over the past two years I had worked very hard in two different jobs and was already quite exhausted when I was exposed to the relentless attacks of Frank, the Administrator. I had been doing two jobs for the salary of one, which did not bother me unduly, knowing that the hospital was always short of money. However, much later when I was shown an account in a financial report, I felt less magnanimous. The man who had been replaced by Frank showed me that over the years when I had been fulfilling the job as Public Relations Director, a substantial salary had been paid out to the man at the top, the Director, for that very job. Now I understood, too, why I could not get any of my requests and complaints further than the outside secretarial office. There was no way for me to get help from the top. It was hermetically sealed and blocked against me.

The heat in my cramped office and resulting perspiration brought on a chest cold which became more and more tenacious. When I had the heart attack, complications set in and eventually embolisms in both lungs were diagnosed. I was in the Intensive Care Unit, being looked after with great care. I knew that I was at death's door. All the indications were there. There were daily prayers and singing outside the ICU by many staff-members of the hospital. The priest came every day. I felt incredibly weak, but was moved to tears by the mountains of flowers, by the love and affection shown to me, not only by the closer circle of my friends, like John, Lux, Joan and Dorothy, but also by the hospital workers – from the engineers to the cooks, nurses, office staff and my volunteers. Their love and affection made me think, but also made me feel so very good in all my pain. 'Maybe I will get out of this after all,' I thought.

Suddenly, one morning, after a dreadful night when my neighbour in the next bed had died, I thought I heard the voice of my mother. 'Don't hate. It is something that will hurt you more than him. It makes you ill and can even kill you. You can turn hate into love.'

What?' I cringed in my contemplation, 'turn my hate for this man into love?' At this moment I felt I would rather kick him in the teeth, if only I had the strength. 'Oh God, I can't!' The thought of my mother's words, however, kept returning to my mind. I knew she was right, and besides, I wanted to live. So I set about changing my feelings. In my mind, I tried to put my hand on his shoulder, saying, 'You must have had a miserable life to have become such a nasty, horrible man!' 'There I go again,' I said to myself. 'Try better!' After I had assuaged the up-welling anger again where I wanted to do him real harm, and where it hurt, I calmed down. 'Come on, Ellen. That's not going to get you anywhere. Try again.' With my hand on his shoulder, I said to him in my mind, 'Maybe your father was a hard man, maybe he kicked you down the stairs when you were a boy to show you that life is a brutal affair.' Now, visualising that little boy, brutalised and helpless, a new feeling swept over me – a feeling of compassion – briefly, but enough to quell the next attack of anger and dislike.

In this way I worked for some days, arriving finally at a stage when I could feel truly sorry for him, knowing suddenly that I could put my arms around him, understanding more clearly than ever that cause and effect have so much to do with how we view the world, ourselves and others. In my mind's world I said to him, 'We can be friends now. I am sorry about my anger and about your problems. I can love you now.'

On that same evening, at around eleven o'clock, the door opened to the darkened ICU room and he came in. He had never come to see me before and I was surprised and curious. He sat down at my bedside and in the dim light from the nurses' desk-lamp, I could see his face. I'd never seen him like this before. His expression was soft and there was an anxious question in his look. Then I became aware of a hopeful little smile reaching from his lips to his eyes. He had noticed my thin, rather crooked smile under the breathing apparatus. I could detect a certain relief when he took my hand gently and, with the bit of strength I had, I gave it a squeeze. Then I noticed what I would never have thought possible: tears were slowly running down his cheeks. He sat there, quietly holding my hand with an expression I can never ever forget. Just beautiful.

I must have fallen asleep then, because when I awoke he had gone. 'Thank you, Mammi,' I said. 'Your advice was good and true.' Love is all we need in this world, I thought, plain miraculous!

As usual, Martin, one of the doctors that I really liked, came in with his entourage of four to do his daily rounds. In turn they listened to my stubborn lungs. 'We are desperately trying to find the virus, Ellen. Bacteriology is working overtime, but so far we haven't been able to pin it down. We're not going to stop till we find it, though. Courage!' I nodded and promptly fell asleep.

That night I had a call from Milan, from my son Tom. The nurses rolled my bed close to their desk to enable me to take the receiver and listen, because I could hardly speak above a whisper. Tom said confidently, 'Mammi, you'll be quite all right. Italy's famous healer, Mr Perotti, will be working for you tonight.' It was wonderful to hear his voice, so sure and comforting. I had a very good night after this conversation and, when the doctor came on his rounds in the morning, I was fast asleep. He took his stethoscope and listened, as usual, to my chest. All of a sudden, his head shot up, his face an expression of utter incredulity. He waved the other doctors over excitedly, asking them to listen. They each in turn listened to my lungs, and each came up with the same look of perplexity. 'Your lungs are free, Ellen, quite clear!' His enormous, broad grin was contagious and spread to everyone around me. Looking at his young doctors, he lifted his shoulders, slightly shaking his head and said, 'Once in a while, miracles happen.'

I realised that I was breathing freely and that I suddenly felt better than I could remember for a long time. My heart, too, was on the mend. I did not want to tell the doctors about the telephone call from Tom, but I was so overjoyed that I reached up with my arms and gave the doctor a big hug. They left me pleased as punch, yet still in a mood of bafflement.

It did not take very long for me to get well enough to leave the hospital. I don't know how I would have survived without my friends, alternating their visits every day. I had met Lux, a child psychologist, a few years previously at an evening class for silk-screen printing. An interesting, generous personality, she fascinated me because she had an outlook on life which was totally positive. I admired her independence, warmth and new ideas. We had many good times together, going to concerts, films, lectures, art exhibitions and occasional meals in each other's apartments. Joan sent me funny, delightful hand-painted cards – one every day. I still have them.

One day, when Dorothy had come down from Pennsylvania to visit, something happened to me. It felt as if a last barrier, already weakened, was pushed down. On her way out she stood in the open door and said, 'Get well, Ellen. You deserve it!' This sentence rang in my ears over and over again. 'Fancy, Ellen,' I said to myself. 'You still find it a bit incredible that you deserve something good.' It rang true, however. I could finally accept it, and myself. The feeling of having such wonderful friends had been a life-line during my illness. Their love and care were a firm basis for lasting friendships.

Just before I fell ill, I had found a beautiful apartment in Queens, right at the border of the forest and the famous tennis courts. I had begun to get it ready, but after all this time in the hospital and the effect of my illness, things had changed. I knew that I could not continue in my career. Tom had entreated me to come to Milan and live with him, his wife Sylvana and their dog Toby. I decided to accept. With John's help, I packed my things and gave away or sold much of the furniture. I was heart-broken to leave my friends, but we all understood that it had to be.

Chapter 19

I WOKE *up feeling happy. The leaves of the high trees in front of my window were swaying gently in the breeze, throwing their shadows around in a lively sun dance. The weather was magnificent. Tempted by the tantalisingly delicious aroma of toast and pancakes, mingled with that of freshly brewed coffee, I went downstairs. Dorothy was just finishing her breakfast. She would have to go shopping with Dolores and Peter, she said. Dolores had just bought a new house in the country. 'We'll be back in two hours or so. Make yourself comfortable in the garden. John called. He'd like to keep you company in the meantime.'*

Dorothy added that he wanted to take us out for a drive and then invite us to dinner at the famous Horseshoe Inn. 'Splendid,' I said, biting into one of Dorothy's delectable pancakes with maple syrup. Dolores and Peter, who had breakfasted earlier, were now arranging the garden furniture on the lawn under the big cherry tree where, later on, we would assemble again for lunch.

After I had cleared up the breakfast dishes, I went into the garden. It was unchanged. The rhododendron bushes, thickly surrounding the house, were in full bloom. A gorgeous wall of light-pink colour – just as I remembered them. Even the raccoons were there, playing on the wide lawn that sloped down to the little river.

I stood still, breathing deeply the fresh and fragrant air, contemplating our friendship that had reached across time and continents. How gently John and Dorothy had made me feel part of their family, giving me a home from home when I first came to this country. I stood in the light which filtered through the trees, letting my eyes wander. The sun was lighting up the flying spray from the sprinklers with all the colours of the rainbow. A dazzling, magnificent display.

I was just going to sit down with my book on one of the deck-chairs when I heard John's unmistakable voice behind me. He had come right into the garden, knowing he would find me there.

After one of his famous bear-hugs, we sat down, pleased to have some time together after so many years. With just the slightest ironical inflection in his voice, he said, 'You're not the world's best correspondent, are you now?'

'True,' I had to admit.

'When, on the rare occasion, a letter arrives from you, Ellen, I am always left with hundreds of questions.'

'Oh, dear, I am really sorry to be such a miserable letter-writer. All I can say – and it's more of an explanation than an excuse – is that I've always disliked writing. I still can't make out why. At the hospital where I had to do a lot of it for my PR work, I managed all right, but I hated it.' Then I added, with a conciliatory smile, 'I hope you will forgive me?'

'You,' he answered in mock indignation, 'are forgiven, but . . . you'll have to pay a penalty.'

'And what would that be, I wonder?' I asked.

'Your penalty would be that you have to tell me, in detail, all about you since you left the States. I have a vague idea from your brief communications that you enjoyed Milan, began painting again, went to live somewhere on the French coast for a while and finally ended up in England where you got married to Leslie. How's that for brevity?' He proceeded to ask me a dozen more questions about the children, my work, England and Leslie. 'He must be quite a guy,' he remarked, 'if you wanted to marry him!

Remember, you said, "I'll never, ever want to marry again." I suppose that was a reaction to your marriage to Mike with his alcohol problem? But, Ellen, most of all, I want to know about your work. Tell me how it developed. Did it grow from what you were doing here at the hospital? Tell me all.'

There was nowhere to start but at the beginning. After leaving New York, I went to join Tom and his wife in Milan. They took me in with open arms, and were so very good to me. This helped enormously in assuaging the pangs of missing my dear friends in New York and all I had grown to love there. Tom thought it would do me a world of good if I would start painting again, so he took me out to buy an easel, lots of oil paints, many canvases and brushes, and then left me to it. He was right. It was a brilliant idea, for I became completely absorbed in the painting and forgot my temporary worries.

I had to work out a technique for oil, as I had only done watercolour and charcoal and sepia thus far. I experimented and really came to love it. To my surprise, I found it much easier than watercolour. The freedom of painting in oil got me quite excited and I started on a series of paintings that I called 'Space Cities'. They were rather dreamlike, sort of fantasy landscapes. They were also in some way quite mystical.

John had asked me if I was inspired by some of the Italian artists, whose works were inevitably all around me in the public buildings of Milan. I felt that I was actually more inspired by Italy itself, the country, the people, just the whole atmosphere of beauty and creativity. It had the effect of unleashing a new wave of creativity in myself. The paintings I did then seemed to have a will of their own. They were so very different from anything I had ever done before.

Tom had rented a lovely little house as a summer residence in the mountains beyond Bergamo. It overlooked an intensely blue lake, surrounded by snow-capped mountains, serene in their ageless beauty. A view to take your breath away. For me, it was sheer inspiration. I was fascinated by the changing light of the day, turning the colour of the lake slowly into an ever deeper incandescent indigo, reflecting the darkening shades of the sky. In the usually clear, deep blue sky one occasionally glimpsed little white puffs of cloud. On some rare occasions, though, a wall of leaden-coloured clouds would form, gathering to warn of one of the violent and explosive deluges, wrapping the whole scene in a shroud of darkness. It never seemed to last long once it had unleashed its fury. Then the sky would clear almost instantaneously, as if swept by a magic brush. Soon, a deep blue sky and air fragrant with ozone and the outpourings of nature's rich and heady scent, surrounded one again.

I remember well the feeling when on an evening I stood in front of the house, breathing in, not just the fresh mountain air, but the incredible beauty of it all, and thought, 'The mountains, the lake, all of it is including me, embracing me. I am part of this!' I loved the place. We went there every weekend, joining the trail fleeing the sooty smell of the city for the health and tranquillity of the country.

I enjoyed living in Milan again, too, sharing some of Tom's and Sylvana's life. It was lovely to sit occasionally in the Galleria with friends, as I had done all those years ago, at a table outside one of those numerous cafés, leisurely watching the elegant Milanese life drift by and letting the rise and fall of exuberant voices and muffled sounds wash over me. It was like background music to our own conversation, reverberating and echoing in the high glass dome of the Galleria.

We revisited our old haunts: quaint trattorias, pizzerias, and the occasional super-elegant restaurant of the *haute-cuisine*. I refreshed my memory and visited the famous Duomo, Milan's fabulous cathedral. As before, the space and beauty of its interior gave me a very special charge. Looking around, I hardly acknowledged the presence of touring groups and their guides giving them information with hushed voices. As when I had come here in the past, I was overcome with the combined impact of so many beautiful works of art in wood, stone and marble, witnesses to generations of people seeking solace and peace here. I thought of the individual artists who, so many years ago, had created their masterpieces here, giving eternal messages of beauty, reaching over the ages to speak of their inspiration to those with eyes to see and a heart to receive.

About six months after my arrival in Milan, I received an invitation to a prize-giving ceremony of an international competition of paintings. I was puzzled and showed it to Tom. He began to laugh, slightly embarrassed, and said, 'Well, since the cat is out of the bag now, I'd better confess. A few months ago I read about this international competition where eighteen nations participated. So I took the painting which you had called "Sinking Venice" from those you had stacked up behind the door, to the collection place with your name and address. I thought it would be fun to see what happens.'

'Oh, Tom! My paintings are only beginner's work. I've only just started in oil!'

'Never mind,' Tom encouraged. 'There's nothing wrong with trying.'

On the day, we all dressed up and went to the ceremony, sitting amongst a crowd of hundreds. The prizes were called out from the stage and the famous television star, Nuccio Costa, was handing over the prizes to the artists, beginning with the hundredth prize. The descent down the numbers progressed ever so slowly, and when it came to about number eighty-eight I thought it might soon be my turn. It continued further and further down and still my name did not come up. I began to think they had made a mistake by inviting me. I heard the droning of the voice, calling out the names, as if from afar, as I slipped into a half-drowsy reverie, lulled by the heat and the murmurings around me. Suddenly I heard, like a trumpet-call, 'Ellen von Einem – Gold Medal'. I looked at Tom, unbelieving, still in my seat. 'Go on, then,' he said, his face as surprised as mine. He ushered me out of the row of chairs and I walked, as if in a dream, to the stage. Nuccio Costa gave me a hug and handed me the Gold Medal for the painting of 'Sinking Venice'. 'Thank you,' was all I could say, disbelief still in my voice. Then, silently, as I made my way back to my seat: 'Thank You, God. But have You got Your tongue in cheek, or did You really mean to give me a break?' We got home in high spirits and celebrated with our friends who had come with us.

It did indeed give me a mighty boost, but I had not reckoned with the avalanche of popularity. I was asked to prepare for an exhibition, I was interviewed on television and radio and by newspaper journalists, and endless invitations to cocktail parties and dinners flooded in. I was overwhelmed and in a real quandary. It was all so sudden and just too much. I pulled myself up and asked the crucial question: 'Where will all this lead to? To another heart attack? No doubt.' I felt it meant a choice between peace and health or hard work and money – lots of it. Making a decision was really not too difficult, though, because I was still feeling quite frail, and the memory of my recent illness was often in my mind. I did not want to go through that again. My choice was made, with one concession: I would do the exhibition, giving myself plenty of time. After that, I'd have to find a hideaway, perhaps somewhere on the Mediterranean, from the place of my newly-found and soon-to-be-lost fame.

Tom took me up into the mountains and there, by myself, during the three weeks I had allocated to it, I painted to my heart's content. The wide open view of the glorious mountains could be seen through the large windows of the downstairs studio-flat and my work was accompanied by the incomparable and inspiring music of Beethoven's symphonies. I forgot time, and often enough food and drink, and produced one painting after another.

On weekends Tom and Sylvana came up from Milan with their young cocker spaniel Toby. He went out of his mind with joy to be there, free and able to run and chase the odd hare. Our neighbouring friends, Enzo and Gemma, were farmers. They supplied us regularly with the necessary food-stuff. I couldn't think of a better life! Enzo and Gemma were also cheese-makers. They showed me around their cellars, filled to the brim with shelves and shelves of wonderful wheels of cheese, reaching up to the ceiling as they sat and matured. I was impressed by the impeccable cleanliness of their place. Going back to Milan, we were always loaded down with all kinds of good, fresh farm produce to take back home with us.

The day of the opening of the exhibition arrived. Nuccio Costa, the handsome actor who had presented me with my Gold Medal, came and opened it, cutting the ribbon in the traditional way. He had bought the painting that won me the gold medal, the one called 'Sinking Venice'. It was an exciting day and a great success. I sold all my paintings but one. I did, however, have tiny pangs of conscience about the half-promises I had given to those who had ordered 'Space City' paintings. The orders had piled up since the receipt of the Gold Medal, and I now had no intention of following them up. I needed to forget about them, completely. All the time, something like a general reassessment of my life, and my life's purpose, was going on in my mind. I was looking forward to my self-imposed 'exile'.

We found a very nice and modern apartment for me, not far from Menton on the Côte d'Azur, in a large apartment building on a wooded hill overlooking the Mediterranean on one side and

From left: Mr Pavone, Tom, myself, Nuccio Costa.
Opening of my exhibition in Milan, 1973.

the forest on the other, palm trees all around. I had no car and I didn't want one. I just wanted to think and enjoy my solitude. I was determined to get back my strength and vitality.

The road on which I lived continued all the way up the mountain through the forest. I made this road my daily exercise. On each bend were several enormous king palms. There I would stop each time to take a breather. The palm-trees – tall, noble, and so beautiful – looked infinitely safe and sound to me. I walked up to the largest of them and put my arms around it, leaning my head against its rather harsh trunk, and murmured, 'You are my strength-giver. You give me hope, dignity and courage. Thank you, king of palms.' As if the tree could hear me, its fronds softly rustled in the wind and, stretching my imagination a bit further, I could hear the rising sap communicating energy and reassurance. However, before greeting my tree friends, I always looked about with care, shy and unwilling to share my moment of enchantment. People watching me might, at best, shake their heads and proclaim that the poor lady was in distress, while the more sober-minded would most probably consider me to be stark raving mad.

Undeterred by such potential judgments, I continued my daily, solitary walks a little further up the mountain every day. My health improved by leaps and bounds. I enjoyed the peace and quiet, contemplating what had happened to me over the years, the changes in my life, in me and around me. The understanding: understanding comes from knowledge, or vice versa? I thought of Kahlil Gibran who had said, 'Pain is the breaking of the shell that encloses your understanding.' Yes, the pain had opened up a fount of knowledge and understanding, answering so many questions and tying up so many loose ends in my mind. I had learned to accept myself, I mused, with all my good points, my talents and abilities, and with all my weaknesses too. I was no more reduced to a zero when someone disapproved of or criticised me. I could, with a level head and detachment, consider criticism for its true merit without letting fly, as if someone had touched a wound, and take it with graceful acceptance.

I noticed something else that had happened over the years: I was not so anxious and concerned any more about what other people seemed to think about me. I felt my own concerns had gradually lost some of their significance. With growing insight and compassion for the pain around me, I experienced a new feeling of connectedness with the rest of the world – with God's Universe. I was filled to the brim with love for all the living. I also realised that my slow transformation was no longer a precarious balance, not to be trusted, but it was here to stay. I could trust that inner teacher, that innermost part of me which, according to Jung's philosophy, connects us to the 'collective unconscious', an archive of knowledge which reveals the truth of all things. Is it identical, I wondered, with the concept of the total wisdom of God? Could I then deduce that God's voice or consciousness was speaking through me? I remembered the dream about the weeds, and I felt that over these years I had been quietly, or not so quietly, pulling away at them, working at eliminating those weeds of self-pity, blaming others and guilt. For now the 'field' around me seemed so much clearer.

Every day when I was walking up the mountain and greeting my wonderful palm trees, I allowed my thoughts free range. Surely there are other weeds to be taken care of? What about pride? I often felt that what we dislike in others can be something we subconsciously recognise and dislike in ourselves, hiding behind a wall of defences: defences like self-righteousness, arrogance or cynicism. 'What about pride then, Ellen?' I asked myself. I had to admit that a lot of the wounds I had been dealt had to do with my pride, my ego. 'I'm still working on it,' I answered. Doesn't it, in the end, all boil down to fear and the insecurity fear creates? People think so often that the best line of defence is attack. Here the memory of the struggle in my sick-bed in the New York hospital, where I turned my hatred of the Administrator into love, overwhelmed me again for the astounding effect it had brought about when I had succeeded. The spotlight had illuminated the cause for many kinds of behaviour and emotions. I realised: 'What we have to do is learn to love.' And with some sadness I thought how many were not as lucky as I in having a role-model to learn from.

Summer had arrived and my health was improving all the time. Marion and my grand-daughter Fiona came to visit me during that sun-filled season. They came by car and by now I was indeed ready to enjoy with them many of the numerous opportunities for entertainment on the Mediterranean coast – village and other festivals galore, and of course, the swimming. I remembered a hidden, beautiful cove, not discovered yet by the madding crowd. The sand and the water were spotlessly clean and dazzling to the eye in their colourful contrast. We went there as often as we could, that is to say on those days when we had no more ambitious plans for the day. Swimming there was heaven. The freshness and clarity of the turquoise blue water had an electrifying effect on us.

Sometimes on weekends Tom and Sylvana came down from Milan to join us. We were the happiest little family alive. To have my dear ones all around me again, as during that marvellous summer in Provincetown, New England, was a real treat. We called the cove 'the jolly cove'. I can't remember having laughed so much and so often, tears running down my cheeks, sides aching, and everyone falling about with mirth. To watch them all in their abandonment, amusing themselves, fancy-free and easy, warmed my heart and again and again I thanked God for granting me my life. My thoughts, with their happiness liberated from the anxiety I had caused them, were able now to appreciate fully what we had all been through in our lives and drink in these moments as from a cup of freedom. I can still feel the exhilaration when I remember those sun-drenched days in Jolly Cove. It was sheer *joie de vivre* – plain happiness.

After a full day on the beach, we would all sit leisurely together on my terrace, enjoying cool drinks and making plans for the next day. It was on one of these occasions when I mentioned that my life here was starting to become a bit boring, and I felt I was ready to get back into a more meaningful life. Much debate followed, with warnings on their part not to become too ambitious, maybe to start painting again in a comfortable, slow-moving way – in short, to play it by ear. Good, sensible advice, I thought. Marion felt that a few weeks with her in England would do me good and could give me the opportunity to have a look around England. Should I not like it, I could always return to my apartment here, but if I decided to stay in England, she would be more than delighted to have me with her as long as I wanted. Her house in Cheltenham was big and there was a room ready for me.

The summer finally came to an end. Marion and Fiona had returned home, looking like pictures of health. Tom came to help me pack and took me to the airport in Nice.

In Cheltenham I began feeling useful again. It was great fun to go into the little forest just behind the house to collect wood for the Aga stove. It also made me feel good to hear English spoken around me. During my first week there, looking out of the window one day, I remarked to Marion, 'It's going to be a lovely day. The sky is almost as blue as on the Mediterranean.'

Marion grinned at me with that subtle smile, an expression around her mouth that always reminded me with a shock of Klaus, and said, 'Let's just wait ten minutes, Mammi, before we come to any rash conclusions.' Indeed, ten minutes later the sky was hung deeply with a curtain of grey.

'No wonder everyone talks about the weather all the time here,' I observed.

'Of course,' she said, smiling widely now. 'You're never at a loss for words.'

Occasionally I got severely reprimanded by my grand-daughter Fiona: 'It's not tomayto,' Mimsey, it is tomahto!' I realised that I had better get rid of the Americanisms that were still part of my language from a habit of many years. She was a surprising child, quite ahead of her age group, with a droll and original way of thinking. Poems she wrote at the age of ten onwards were of astounding maturity and quality. I had no idea why she called me Mimsey, but that was what she did already at three years old. Our love for each other has never faltered. She has had to cross many bridges too and has reached the other side more positive than ever, charming and warm-hearted.

For seven years Marion had lived in a quiet country place not far from Gloucester. She had withdrawn from her former busy town-life after the divorce from Sean, to find peace and herself again with her little daughter Fiona. She began to develop her considerable talents for sculpture and other artistic expressions.

At that time Marion got engaged to a local builder. They were going to get married soon, but before that she had to undergo an operation, a long-standing problem that finally had to be sorted out. During my stay in Birmingham, where Marion had been taken for the operation, I met some dear, long-lost friends, Helen, Anthony and their son Sam. They insisted that I stay with them during my time in Birmingham and as long as I wanted. When I told them that I was hoping to find a cottage somewhere in the country, they suggested that I come to Shropshire. They were in the process of buying a house there and thought perhaps I should have a look around in that part of the country. 'It's an area of great natural beauty,' they assured me.

Marion was getting better fast. I had been visiting her in the hospital every day and Robin, her fiancé, had prepared everything for the wedding. It was a small church ceremony and, after a lively reception which I organised, they both went off happily to Cheltenham. Fiona had only been given two days' leave from her boarding school and had to return immediately.

Helen and Anthony had concluded the purchase of their house in Ludlow and I promised to come and see them as soon as I returned from a visit to Germany which I had been planning for some time. When I finally arrived there by bus, I found the journey down to Ludlow over the Clee Hill enchanting. They had made their home most enjoyable and eminently comfortable and, once there, I was really eager to explore the countryside and find a place to live, close to nature, but not too far from the amenities.

After several unsuccessful efforts, the housing agent sent us to a little town near the Welsh border. Driving through the wooded valley of incomparable beauty, we arrived at the place nestling on a hill with quaint old houses leaning onto each other along the High Street. Finally, we found Fields Cottage and my excitement increased. From the bottom of the town, behind the old church, a dirt road led up the hill and there, supremely placed, was Fields Cottage, surrounded by thousands of huge daffodils. I could hardly believe my eyes. I wanted to live here, in a country of such gentle beauty, unspoiled and totally captivating with its views over the valley and hills beyond. Breathtaking! 'Here,' I thought, 'amongst these gentle hills as old as time, I can be at peace, find a permanent new home' (Fields Cottage was just a rented house) 'and allow myself the luxury of leisurely putting myself together again. Here I can really make a new life.'

Friends and family came to visit me there. Everyone was enthusiastic, feeling the beauty of the place, completely captured by the peace and quiet. I enjoyed long months on my own and the occasional visitors were a welcome interruption of my solitude.

My neighbour, Margie, lived next to my cottage (there were only three houses on this part of the hill). She would sometimes come in for a chat and a cup of tea, offering her help for several hours during the week to do some cleaning. Below, halfway down the hill, lived one of the local grocers with his wife and dog. They were hard-working people who had started out with a small grocery shop and ended up with a flourishing little supermarket. Every evening they came by, walking their enormous dog and their friendly greetings led to a lengthy chat, and often a cup of tea. These were the first inhabitants I met in my new environment, and they made me feel good and accepted. My contact with them helped me to gain a bit of insight into the ways and characteristics of these kindly Shropshire people.

I was able to achieve with my little rented cottage all that I had hoped and envisaged. The few pieces of antique furniture I was able to acquire in Birmingham, together with some practical bits and pieces I found in my little town, fitted in just right with the rest of the furniture already there. Some beautiful plants graced the row of windows overlooking the valley. I was as pleased as punch.

One spring day my beautiful room was flooded with the morning sun pouring through the open windows. I heard the doorbell and went to open the door. It was the vicar's wife. She welcomed me so warmly and was so genuinely friendly that I took to her immediately. During the course of our conversation, she asked if I would like to accompany her and her husband on one of their walks over the hills. 'It's bluebell time, you know,' she added. 'There's a special treat waiting!'

We made an appointment for the next day. To my surprise and joy, the weather held and in the balmy spring air we set out over the hills, the sun bringing out the best in all creation. We had to pass from the cottage along a tiny path, occasionally scratched by unruly twigs from the hazelnut trees bordering the path. Climbing across stiles and walking over cow-pat-dotted meadows, we were lazily observed by a multitude of cows, following our progress with huge, unfathomable eyes, undisturbed and infinitely at peace with themselves and the world, chewing the cud. The last of the stiles led into a forest, descending to a rushing brook at the bottom of the valley. I gasped at the sight. A carpet of bluebells stretched throughout the valley with an intense, vibrating blue. I had never seen anything like it – such an abundance of flowers. Roy and Hannah watched my amazed expression and I told them that the treat they had promised surpassed all that my imagination could have envisaged.

My friends from Ludlow came one day, bringing some of their friends whom I had met with them in Birmingham. They felt that it was time for me to get a car again. I agreed. I was ready to do some exploring. Their encouragement, and the car, were just what I needed. They located a little Renault 4 for me, second hand, from their Renault dealer at a good, affordable price for me, and I christened her Bluebird.

In the meantime Marion and Robin had moved to London, and in December 1976 a little boy was born: Benjamin. When they came to see me, he was only a few weeks old. Holding him in my arms, this tiny new life had the effect of giving me new life too. It was only six months earlier, in May, that Tom had given me the good news of the birth of Raffaele, his little son. Now there were two additions to our family. I thought of their ages, so close together, and hoped they would be friends.

I explored the hills and valleys surrounding me on my own and with my new and old friends. Walking here not only opened my heart, but also opened up the countryside to me in all its differing moods under a vast sky, transforming its rural beauty from hour to hour. It felt as if a magnificent book was revealing its closely-held secrets.

I took to my new homeland like a duck to water. My longing to go back to the country where I was born had always been with me as long as I could remember. I wondered if my fondness for the south Shropshire landscape was because it reminded me in an uncanny way of New Zealand. I don't know. I was only a little tot when we left, but I am quite willing to assume that it had to do with my feelings of having come to rest, having come home.

I began to paint again. Two exhibitions in nearby towns told me I had not wasted my time. My paintings in oil and water-colour sold well and had given me much satisfaction and joy.

For some time I had been seeing a chiropractor because of a long-standing problem with my back. As a young girl and vigorous athlete, I had injured it, diving from the high spring-board. It had left my back vulnerable, and every now and then I needed treatment. In New York I had found out that the best results were achieved by a good chiropractor.

The night before my last scheduled appointment with the chiropractor, who lived about twenty miles away, I had another of those intensely clear and vivid dreams: I was on my way to the chiropractor in Bluebird when I saw a red mail van come down a wooded lane on my right. The driver, halfway leaning out of the window, gallantly waved me on. I could clearly see his face, his ginger hair and moustache in every little detail. In my dream, I remember thinking, 'What a nice face.'

I awoke with a start, the sharp image of the postman's face clearly in my mind. I got out of bed and walked around for a while, puzzled at the strange intensity of the dream. I just couldn't see any meaning in it. Until the next day. On my way to my appointment, Bluebird behaved rather oddly. She kept stalling and made strange noises. I contemplated taking her into the next garage, but did not listen to my better sense and felt that it was more important to get to my appointment on time and have it over with. Even if I had to limp there, I would keep on going.

As I came onto a long stretch of road, I suddenly saw the red van, exactly as it appeared in the dream. It was appearing from the same wooded lane on the right. I stopped, goose-pimples rising on my arms. The ginger-haired man waved me on in the same gallant way as he had in my dream. I stared at him with shock. This was a precise repetition of the dream in every detail. I just sat there until he motioned me on again with a broad smile, and I drove on, shaking my head in confusion.

Jung would tell me: 'Take notice of your dreams. They can contain messages from your subconscious, messages expressed by symbol.' Yes, I thought, the message must mean 'stop'. The red van meaning a red light, perhaps. But the dream was obviously prophetic, and I couldn't explain that. All I could do, I felt, was go slowly. So I did. I carried on driving at about thirty-five miles an hour. When I came around a downhill bend, I saw a big truck racing up towards me on my side of the road. At that moment there was no escape. The verge on my side was steep and I could only go so far to the left. As the truck passed, it caught the back of Bluebird as it raced on. Bluebird turned over and over again. Inside, I held on to the wheel as if my life depended on it, which it did. Never letting go of the wheel, I bounced around in the car, hitting the roof and the sides until at last the car and I ended up in a pile sideways.

I was knocked out and was just coming to as somebody tried to get me out of the car. I remember little else and regained consciousness again in the care of two nurses in the hospital who were looking down on me. I ached all over. I could not move my head nor my legs.

It was some time before I even felt like moving, intensely fearful that perhaps I had lost the ability to do so. One of the nurses, obviously seeing my concern, said, 'Let's see if you can walk.' God, I thought, I'd like to know that too – desperately!

With a supreme effort, clenching my teeth with the pain around my chest, I moved with the help of both nurses out of bed and, with an inner cry of joy and an outer stream of tears, I ventured out, one step at a time. I silently sent up my thanks – saved, once more.

It wasn't long before I was back home. I had broken three ribs, each in several places, and had suffered a concussion. I knew I would soon be right as rain, but berated myself for not having heeded the warning, in retrospect so clear. Even Bluebird had tried to warn me, I thought. Now my back was as bad as it had been when I started my chiropractic treatments and poor Bluebird was no more. For a while I would just have to take the bus.

One day, about a week after the accident, the telephone rang and a rich, warm voice at the other end of the line inquired about my recovery from the accident. 'Who are you?' I asked, slightly bemused.

'A friend of your gardener,' he said. 'He has been working for me for many years, and he says that he is your gardener too.'

'Oh, yes, Cecil, you mean, the friendly gardener? Of course, he has told me a lot about you. You are the man who built his own observatory in his garden and has also made the telescope for it.'

'True, But I really wanted to know if I could help you in any way. Do you need anything?'

He offered to come up and see me and I told him that I would enjoy that. I asked him if he had any parsley and chives, which he did, and he arrived the very next day with a huge bouquet of them – enough to supply a hotel for a week.

The bearer of the herbs was a charming and interesting man. Cecil had called him 'The Astronomer' and had told me about his travels around the world, and about the tragic death of his young second wife a year previously. It seems we hit it off instantly. I had the most entertaining and fascinating afternoon. Leslie had been widowed twice, as I had, although my second husband died a year after our divorce. We saw quite a lot of each other after that first meeting. Needless to say, we spent much of our time telling each other about our lives.

He had developed an interest in astronomy at an early age, inspired by his mother. Like many others in the 1960s, he was a keen observer of lunar and planetary phenomena and became particularly interested in astro-photography. He built an observatory to house his large telescope, to which an ordinary camera was attached. However, he became very frustrated by the delay involved in taking pictures of the stars in constantly changing atmospheric conditions, often having to wait weeks to get his pictures back from the developer. He therefore decided to study the possibility of adapting a then existing method of photography like the Polaroid method for use with the telescope to cut out the delay. It involved designing and constructing a series of special cameras over a period of two years. Eventually he achieved success, and for the first time instant pictures of space were obtained. The result was published and for this development he was elected a Fellow of the Royal Astronomical Society. Lectures followed and Leslie formed lasting friendships with many well-known members of the astronomical fraternity. In their company he visited the great observatories in the United States where interest in his work had been expressed.

He invited me to lunch one day. It was a culinary feast. He had become an accomplished cook during those years after his first wife's death. They were seven long years of loneliness, trying to adjust to the loss of his life-time companion, the mother of his two sons. He showed me through his house which, in some way, reminded me of the home in Leipzig where I grew up, if only in the large size of the rooms, the thick walls and high ceilings, and in the marvellous spacious kitchen – pantries, storage rooms galore and a splendid Rayburn oven taking pride of place. All over the place I could detect the signs of an ingenious spirit, uncannily thought-out improvements, remedial attachments, whole pieces of furniture for the purpose of making life easier for the home-maker, designed and built by Leslie.

Seven years after his first wife had died of cancer he married a young and beautiful woman suffering from an incurable disease. He was touched by her courage and genuine sweetness and, with deep love and compassion, he was able to give her seven months of happiness before she died.

I was recovering fast from the accident, aided by the opportunity to share ideas and to communicate with a like-minded spirit with an understanding and stimulating mind. One breezy spring morning, he appeared at the doorstep, laden with an enormous bunch of glorious roses. He wanted to ask me something, he said. I led him to his favourite seat by the window opposite mine and, after he had settled down comfortably, he said very quietly, as if no one else but me must hear it, 'Would you marry me?'

Over the past weeks I had been in a bit of a quandary just in case this question might come up. I kept thinking of my decision never to get married again, to which I had stuck so far. On the other hand, here I had encountered a kindred spirit, a companionable man to whom I felt drawn with a new sense of trust. I needed to think about it and asked for a little time.

Pondering about the 'yes' and 'no' for quite a while, I eventually came to the conclusion that we could, if we both tried, build a life together and be companions to each other instead of facing lonely years ahead. Soon after we were married in the local church by our mutual friend, the vicar.

It seemed to me that Leslie's house welcomed me. Or was that wishful thinking? No, it was as if I could hear the place entreating me to brighten up its sadness. Leslie's family, too, welcomed me into their fold with open arms. I felt grateful and lucky, and with the knowledge and wisdom of hindsight, I can say it was one of the best decisions I made in my life. Leslie, too, reached out to my children and family with love and, for the first time, my children had a father-figure and my grand-children a grandfather. The strong family-sense in both families made for harmonious relations.

Leslie, c.1990.

With his artistic and yet down-to-earth practical approach to almost any task at hand, Leslie tackled the construction of a pool in his garden, fulfilling the wish of Audrey, his first wife. He chose an ideal place for it on the lawn in front of the house that was encircled by the drive. With the help of the gardener, they dug out the earth in a pear shape and the bottom and walls of the pool were so thoroughly cemented that in the many years since its creation, the pool has held its water without a leak, withstanding the sharpest frost.

Leslie also constructed a sloping, fifteen-foot wall along the drive with some huge sandstone blocks made available when the old market hall was pulled down nearby. On the lawn side of it, he built a rockery with pointed stones at the top above the wall, representing his vision of the Matterhorn and the high peaks of Mont Blanc. Next he installed a powerful electric pump to raise the flow of water twelve feet above the pool so that it cascaded down a series of waterfalls into several pebble-filled little pools before dropping into the main pool below. A pump also supplied a small fountain, spraying its water over a charming little statue of a girl gazing down into the pool from a small rocky island.

I loved this pool and spent many hours reading and swinging on our garden swing seat just beside it. Once when my grandchildren were visiting, it was time for the pool to be cleaned. The excitement could be heard a mile away, I'm sure. Every now and then a delighted cry: 'A newt, a newt!' came from Fiona who had the task of filling a pail of fresh water with the frogs and newts as the water-level sank. Raffaele and Ben had to carry away the accumulated slush from the bottom of the pool, and the whole affair was conducted with the utmost sense of importance and noise, Leslie directing, encouraging the work-gang with praise or, at times, with a word of admonishment. Watching them from the lounge, I had happiness in my heart.

At night the pool was floodlit and we often sat outside enjoying the coolness of the evening, with the melodic splashing sound of the fountain and the peace after a hot day.

Light and brightness was spreading through the house. It had come to life again. A new heating system was installed and the few pieces I had brought along fitted in well with the existing furniture. The sun-lounge, which had also been built onto the house many years before and had been designed in great detail by Leslie, was given a new lease of life too. A small sofa and seats which I had acquired for the cottage and covered with a colourful, striking material, made the sun-lounge bright and inviting. It became our favourite spot to sit.

Leslie and I enjoyed our life together, in spite of the inevitable ups and downs and the occasional misunderstandings. We'd lived long enough to know about the perils of adjustment. There had to be a lot of give and take. We came to know each other's vulnerabilities and strengths and as life went on, our trust and respect for each other continued to grow. There seemed never to be a dull moment; time slipped by unnoticed.

The evenings were spent telling each other of the many experiences we had had. Leslie had gone to Bourne College, a boarding school at Quinton, near Birmingham. Quinton was a pleasant village, but Leslie hated the surrounding Black Country. After he was finished there he never wanted to see another factory chimney again. He happily returned home to be the fifth generation learning the tailoring trade and eventually take over the long-established business from his father, although his interests lay far more along scientific lines.

When the First World War broke out, his hopes of being accepted as a pilot in the RAF were dashed owing to astigmatism in both eyes. Instead, although still under age, he enlisted in the Royal Naval Air Services as a motorcycle dispatch rider, and was posted to Scapa Flow in the Orkney lslands on a balloon station. There, submarine spotting was in operation to safeguard supply convoys and protect the fleet from attack.

After his return from the war, he was sent to the London Tailor and Cutter Academy and received his diploma in due course. He had to take over the family business in a hurry, owing to his father's severe illness. He soon learned to handle the business, the numerous employees and the shop. He bought a second shop not long after and had soon established himself as a respected tailor of class and distinction. His clientele came from all over England, Scotland and Ireland.

Owing to his artistic bent, he was able to create elegant suits and garments for people with high demands, and he could also enhance a less than perfect figure, balancing out – almost sculpturing, in a way – a suit for the unfortunate body, hiding its shortcomings.

In his twenties, Leslie built his own short-wave radio set, to become one of the first to listen to transmissions from the United States and from Melbourne, Australia. From then on he began to build and install all the radio sets in the town and surroundings. With the proceeds he bought himself a motorcycle to roam around Europe on many a holiday.

The sun was rising ever higher and, all the while I had been talking, John had been listening with total concentration and interest. Pulling over the shade to better protect us from the glaring sun, he took my hands and said with warmth, 'Thank you with all my heart, Ellen, you have now paid the penalty in full.' He took me in his arms and once more I enjoyed that wonderful bear hug of his and felt the old bond of friendship renewed.

It was perfect timing. Suddenly we heard excited voices as Dorothy and the two marriage candidates returned from their shopping trip, pleased with their new acquisitions. Together we all prepared a light and delicious lunch and sat down in the warmth of the sun, and of our friendship, to eat.

Chapter 20

Over the years together, our life has settled down in a harmonious rhythm, affording me the opportunity and time to develop and enjoy my other interests. I painted a lot and continued my long-standing deep fascination with psychology and spirituality. Reading, studying and taking various courses seemed to fill the extra time.

One day, about a year after we had married, my former neighbour, Margie, came to see me. We had kept in touch and saw each other occasionally. With her was a girl, Sally, who was in trouble. Margie thought I might be able to help. 'She is catatonic – in shock,' I thought immediately.

'Her parents are my friends,' Margie told me.

Looking at her, my first reaction was that she should be taken to the hospital. I did not know how I could help her and told Margie this. Margie pleaded with me. 'Every time the hospital is mentioned, Sally gets panicky and wildly over-excited.'

Sally was trembling. 'Why don't you want to go there?' I asked her. 'You will surely get help from a kind doctor.' She just stared at me with huge, entreating eyes. She could not speak when she tried. Her movements were wooden and limited, as if her body had stopped functioning.

'Someone has to help her, Ellen, and I couldn't think of anyone else who could do it in a way that would not harm her. I agree with her parents. They really don't want her taken away and drugged. Your method is very gentle, I know, and loving.'

Unsure of what to do or say, I asked to be excused for a

moment, and went into my study. There I prayed, asking for a clear answer to Margie's plea. It came so fast, and clearly, I felt I had received an answer and a vital charge of energy. My mind was suddenly quite reassured. I felt strongly that I should try and that I would have support.

I went back into the room and told Margie that I would give Sally counselling and later on, if successful, I would consider some deep relaxation. The relief on Margie's face was quite a sight. When I looked at Sally, she seemed to have slowly come to life. There appeared to be just the hint of a smile on her face, though her eyes were still fearful. I took her warmly into my arms, spontaneously, overwhelmed by the sadness coming from her. 'Shall we let Margie have a chat with Leslie, and then we can have one together? What do you think?' She nodded and Margie left us to ourselves.

I could see that she was quite unable to speak, but she was listening. The expression on her face was gradually relaxing. I talked about anything that came to mind in a lighthearted, relaxed way, sometimes jokingly, and always reassuringly – a kind of self-answering dialogue.

By the end of about an hour, she began to speak for the first time in two weeks. I felt that she had suffered from a psychological shock and decided on an intensive series of treatments in order not to lose the advantage gained. She came almost every day for a fortnight, when I gave her counselling and later deep relaxation.

Sally responded well, coming more and more to life. Her paralysis, her paranoic fears, the shaking of her body, gradually subsided, and she began to move and speak normally. After about ten sessions, she began to write poems of great beauty and reading them out to me gave her much joy. We could then easily discuss her feelings and work on positive thinking, and on her problems (childhood traumas). I later saw quite a few people who came for counselling, particularly for stress relief and marital problems, but I never again encountered such a drastic case.

I was delighted to have been able, with God's help, to release Sally from the trauma. She learned to use her exceptionally beautiful voice with a well-known musician. Together they have completed their second album successfully, and are now happily married and living on the Mediterranean.

Sally later wrote to me, telling me of her experiences through our sessions together. She spoke of the 'great safety' she felt when we first met, and how important it was to her at the time to be able to trust someone. 'After the first session,' she wrote, 'I felt that at least half of the burden had lifted,' and that through our work together she found many of the answers to 'questions I had been searching for an answer to physically, mentally and spiritually. You helped me to find myself, but most of all, you gave me invaluable teachings to refer to, to maintain a happy life.'

After Sally's happy recovery, the word somehow spread and the number of people coming for help increased and eventually snow-balled to such an extent that I felt unable to handle it any more. I had to say, 'No, sorry!' My priority had to remain with Leslie, my husband.

When I was approached, one day, by a member of a BBC radio station, and asked for an interview, I felt that I had to refrain as it would no doubt lead to an increase in the number of people seeking help. The interviewer suggested: 'Why don't you do a course to teach your method to others who might be interested in helping people in the way you do?' I thought about that for a moment and said, 'That is really a very good idea. Why didn't I think of that myself?' I arranged to do the interview and we discussed the course along with my beliefs about a loving, gentle form of therapy, which I had decided to call Attitudinal Therapy with Deep Relaxation. As a result of the broadcast, I received quite a few calls.

I was now confronted with the task of putting together my ideas and the technique of my therapy into a kind of teachable order. I set about writing a series of talks on different aspects of life and my thoughts on them. I found someone to help with the course who had some experience of such things. She put together an interesting array of experiential exercises and some games to lighten the hours and create ease and lots of laughter.

The first course took place every Saturday for ten weeks, and the sessions covered such topics as: Love and Forgiveness, Self-sufficiency and Self Reliance, Discovering and Dealing with Problems, Stress and Relaxation, and Personal Transformation, as well as the Techniques of Attitudinal Therapy. It was fully booked with ten students and turned out to be a success. Many others followed over the years and are still going on.

It seems to me now that the ideas that created Attitudinal Therapy emerged slowly in my mind over time, stimulated by the various life experiences and lessons I had. The work I did with young people in New York was the catalyst that started me laying the foundations of what I do now. There I was able to test the effectiveness of my beliefs, and the warm response of those wonderful youngsters gave me the strength and conviction to go on.

I came to realise more and more just how important and directional our attitudes really are. They rule our lives. A great man said: 'This whole life is a challenge to growth. That is true religion and psychology, because a true religion cannot be other than a true psychology . . . it gives you a great challenge to be more than you are now. It gives you a divine discontent. It makes you want to go higher – not higher than others, but higher than yourself.'

We all experience an opposition at times between being ourselves and meeting the projected expectations and requirements of other people, for example, our families (even long after we have left them), friends, colleagues and authority figures. It appears that to become ourselves, we have to build up ego, but in order to connect with others we have to repress or overcome ego. One has to work on that conflict to look for a way in which we can meet other people and the world around us without having to sacrifice our uniqueness.

I can give an example of someone who came to see me. Her mother had recently died and, as in so many instances like this, there were many things left unsaid, many instances which caused pain to my client and which she desperately wished to resolve between herself and her mother. During the deep relaxation session we visualised her meeting her mother and dealing with some of these issues in a secure environment.

The therapy session would have gone something like this: after some counselling and having reached a state of deep relaxation by consciously relaxing each part of the body in turn, I would begin.

'Imagine yourself resting on a mossy bank in a lovely wood. It is summer, the shadows of the leaves above you are playing over your face and body, and a gentle breeze is caressing you. You are completely relaxed and enjoying the beauty around you. After a while you see someone coming towards you through the wood. As she draws nearer you recognise your mother. You motion for her to come near and sit down. You are both pleased to see each other. You feel able to tell her all the things that have been bothering you over the years. Looking at her, you see an expression of deep sorrow. She tells you how hard it was for her to do or be otherwise, of the struggles she had in her own youth and the efforts she made to do things right. You feel stirrings of compassion, and suddenly you realise that everything is cause and effect. Just as you are suffering from the way she behaved, so she suffered from the actions of her parents, and so on. Through your growing understanding and compassion, you realise that you are sisters in pain. Your heart is full of forgiveness and in your new understanding, you both hug each other. All the pain melts away – yours and hers, and you can both smile again.'

In this case, the client felt a marked difference in her feelings towards her late mother after the session. She said it was really as if she had in fact met her mother and talked about these things in peace and harmony. Because of this healing, she was then able to improve her own self-image.

Deep relaxation with guided imagery brings about an awareness of the immense power that transcends us all and the whole of the universe. Opened up to its current, its pulse, coming from the source of all life, infinitely creative and totally unconditional in its giving, we begin to realise that we don't have to do it all alone; we do have help. We are guided and protected when we open up to that help. The blocks in our lives, created mostly in our childhood, programme us to say, 'I can't.'

Can we forgive ourselves and others? Yes, we can. We can allow ourselves to receive of the abundance, given unconditionally by the source of life, God, that creative force which wipes out our paralysis, our fears and resentments, lighting the fire of knowledge, of our own ability to choose: to choose how long we want to suffer; to choose what to think; to choose to love ourselves as we are, with all the good and all the bad, even if others do not love us. We are creators; we create our own life. We come to understand that our parents were not perfect, but they were the perfect challenge for us to grow.

As we identify our patterns of behaviour, of feelings and thoughts, including the obvious and hidden, we can create a new image of ourselves. We can choose to accept our parents, children, friends, relatives, in our relationships, as they really are, and we can now allow ourselves to be who we are. We can set them free and set ourselves free. This freedom permits true peace, harmony and independence and is the first step towards a truly authentic way of living.

These and other thoughts were amongst those I expounded to John on the lawn that day, no doubt telling him more than he possibly wanted to know. And I listened too to his stories about his own journey, glad that our paths had crossed once more.

Chapter 21

Over the years the contact with Kiki's children had remained alive and when I recently received an invitation to visit Terraqueuse on my way to a holiday in Spain, I could not resist it. I stopped over in Paris to stay a few days with my son Tom and his two children, Raffaele, seventeen and Sandy, nine, which is always a very special joy and treat for me, as we are very close and inevitably much fun and celebrating is going on.

These visits are doubly exciting for me, as I can look forward to my return journey when I can stop over in Englefield-Green near Windsor to see my daughter Marion and my grandson Ben. Enough to warm the cockles of a mother's heart!

In Paris Tom and I had been invited for dinner in Chantal's exquisitely beautiful apartment. The Eiffel Tower was looming gracefully and huge right in front of our eyes, across the terrace. Three of Kiki's daughters, Flo and her husband Jean Pierre, Bea and Chantal were there, and Bea had lovingly prepared a splendid meal.

Chantal now spends her days in the hospital where her husband Dr Raymond Roi-Camille, a famous orthopaedic surgeon, is fighting a battle for his life – a struggle Chantal lovingly and intimately shares with him. It is a heavy burden, which she carries with great fortitude. It was lovely to see her again and it was also a surprise – she had evolved into a woman of great presence and warmth.

Flo, the youngest, was the sunshine of the family, who had always possessed a talent to see the bright side of life – and people. Sweet and gentle, unchanged and positive, she can make people happy just by being herself. Now, with her four children at an age to relieve her of the most urgent duties of motherhood, she seems to have developed, unknown to herself, undercover as it were, a marvellous talent as a painter. She was taken by surprise with an insatiable thirst to paint – paint – paint. I could not believe my eyes – nor could anyone else – when she produced one beautiful painting after another. Exhibitions followed and critiques which appreciate the sheer *joie de vivre* her paintings exude.

Kiki's second oldest daughter, Bea, a thoughtful and interesting personality, had experienced deep hurts in her life and with great courage has found her way out of pain and disillusionment – overcoming many hurdles which could have destroyed others.

I sent my thoughts out into the ether wondering if they would be received: 'Kiki, have you been observing your children? Are you proud that each one of them has stood up to the vagaries of time and life in the spirit you imparted to them, through your life on earth, so splendidly?'

It was a pity that I could not see the rest of the family: Dolky, Boby and Kalou with their families, but I think and hope there will be other occasions.

I travelled on to Terraqueuse the next day. The family was enjoying the end of the Easter holiday there. An amicable family solution had been found to maintain the happy holiday tradition of the ever-growing family after Kiki's death. Although living in Toulouse, Phillippe was the owner now and in charge of Terraqueuse. Jacqueline, his lovely wife, has a truly momentous task to step into Kiki's shoes as the silent organiser of all and the creator of a happy atmosphere during the holidays – and how well she lives up to it!

On my first day there, I was impressed: everything had remained as it was when I saw it last. The warmth of their welcome and their interest in my life and work was touching. The three days there went far too quickly. I walked around my old hunting grounds then out through the entrance-gate, where the view took my breath away. In the distance – all along the horizon – the Pyrenees! Snowcapped mountains under a cloudless sky! I had forgotten about this rare sight. I walked back into the grounds and my feet carried me to the area of the swimming pool. Suddenly I was transported back in time: hearing Kiki's happy voice and the hubbub and sound of excited joyous children. Laughter, shrieks of delight and horror, the splashing of water and the rhythmic thump-thump of tennis balls. I had to squeeze my eyes to come back to this time in May. In July and August all will be like that again, I thought, when one or the other of these young ones then, will be back as a mother herself.

Jacqueline picked me up at the airport in Toulouse and we recognised each other immediately. I got to know her so much better on this occasion – and was glad I had come. Her naturalness and sincerity were captivating and the care and affection she gave me made me feel welcome and loved. Both Jacqueline and Phillippe had survived almost fatal illnesses which, obviously, gave their lives, now healthy again, a totally new meaning.

The number of people around the big dining table, which I remembered so well, was much reduced, with my hosts, myself and two of their children: Valeri, nineteen, a serious and charming young lady, Emanuel, nine, and three friends of Valeri. They were a year younger than her and had come to Terraqueuse to study for their impending A-Levels (Baccalauréat). I think that Valeri gave them the benefit of her knowledge, having passed her exams the previous year. They were tired at the end of three weeks' intensive cramming – and I think, they enjoyed the chance of some light relief. Sincere and lively, they tried their English occasionally on me – creating enough cause for leg-pulling and laughter.

Emanuel is a delightful young chap with an inborn assurance

and dignity which does not hinder his bright and enthusiastic disposition. Showing me around the estate, he explained everything clearly and intelligently, gallantly tolerating my lamentable French and, on my request, teaching me words in French for certain trees and plants.

We arrived eventually in the midst of a flock of sheep in a field (thank goodness for my wellies!), when he suddenly started to run, crying back to me: 'A lamb has hung itself up on its leg!'

For a while I could not see it, till I came nearer to the pen. There indeed was the poor little lamb, stuck with one of its feet trapped between two boards of the fence, fairly high up. God only knows how long it had been hanging there. We worked hard to release the pressure, straining to pull apart those boards; they did not want to budge. We had to open them up enough to pull out the foot. It took quite some time and in the end we succeeded with a loud 'Yuppeee!'

'Chapeau!' I said, 'I am in the company of a hero, you are a champ! Without you spotting that little lamb, and without your strong arms – it would have died! I am glad,' I told him, 'that I was there to help you – but I am sure, even without me you would have tackled the situation in the right way.' He gave me a rather lovable smile – he had understood the meaning of my poor French.

Then he gallantly and companionably took my hand to lead me over some wet paddy and squeaky ground. At the dining table – dinner was just ready to be served, when we returned – he excitedly recounted the experience and for once he had the ear of everyone.

I learned about one change they had made and congratulated Jacqueline and Phillippe on their practical and wise decision to make part of the castle available for paying guests during the summer months. It has, quite obviously, worked out to everyone's advantage.

When Phillippe took me back to the airport it was with a new sense of friendship that we parted. I was very happy to have revisited Terraqueuse and to have again met more members of this remarkable family.

Soon after I got home again I had news from Chantal. Raymond, her husband, had lost his battle. Or won it, I thought? Did he not walk through that door to the other side of life – into freedom – into light? Chantal's pain is profound and lonely, as it is for any one of us who are left by our beloved.

The healing power of love, the warmth and compassion of family and friends, takes on a deeper meaing than at any other time.

Chapter 22

THAT trip to New York was made some years ago now. The time with John and Dorothy was filled with more memorable dinners, walks and warm exchanges of humour and affection. It was with many bitter-sweet feelings that I parted from them that spring, not knowing when we would see each other again.

Now, back in Shropshire, I am having to slow down a little. I am only doing one course a year now, and have only a couple of clients. But the work continues through many of my students since the first course. These include social workers, nurses and other therapists. They find that Attitudinal Therapy with Deep Relaxation enhances their practice. The courses also seem to have created a wonderful circle of like-minded people. We occasionally have reunions where the students of different courses come together. These days are always warm and full of laughter. I have been fortunate, too, in gaining some very special and dear friends through these opportunities to share my ideas, for whom I am immensely grateful.

My thoughts venture out to the great value of friendship. I have recently read an article in which three women wrote about their 'Best Friend'. It made me think. My best friend is Renate Stegmaier. We have seen each other no more than three times during the last twenty years, or more. Yet this friendship does not seem to have very much to do with being together – or even with an intensive correspondence (ours is sporadic – at times, even non-existent!), but with an extraordinary connectedness which is spiritual and enduring. But, when we can get together, it is most rewarding and becomes one of those highlights in life. I am looking forward to seeing her again next year, in 1995, in the little town of Giengeu a.d. Brenz in Suabia, where my parents settled after the war.

Friendship is a great part of our life – and my mind is drifting to one remarkable woman who I am happy and proud to call a very dear friend. I met Mary Walsh when she was at a crossroads. After she had attended one of my early workshops she seemed to have slipped out of a 'chrysalis', unfolding her wings in an extraordinary way. From being a social worker, unhappy and unfulfilled, she gradually developed her inherent skills and became part-owner of an agency for abused children. They now own four houses, have over thirty staff, and Mary is in great demand to speak at conferences all over the world. Her noteworthy technique to deal with this worldwide problem is held in great esteem to combat one of the greatest threats of our time. With a heart of pure gold and a brilliant mind for practical organisation she is giving many unhappy children a new lease of life.

Looking back over this strange and interesting life of mine, it may seem that I fell into the same traps many times until I fully learned what I had to learn. However, I sincerely believe that nothing is ever lost. Everything that happened to me released new knowledge and a deeper understanding, and I can never stop marvelling at an infinitely wise and forgiving spirit behind it all. This spirit which, after feeling its presence clearly and, at times, dimly, I call God, seems to have coerced and pushed me along, sometimes into apparent chaos and near self-destruction. It has been a journey through tunnels of darkness, self-doubt, guilt and deep anger, emerging into moments of sheer light and awareness with flashes, like flares sent up into the night sky to brighten the search for the lost ship.

It was when I had lost faith in myself, others and God Himself

– in short, when I hit rock-bottom – that suddenly things changed. Something happened:

GRACE. I was given grace again and again. A shaft of light, seemingly from nowhere, broke through into the darkness of my soul, working wonders of reconciliation and opening many windows of my mind.

In profound wonderment I perceived the truth of the divinity of life, and that both the profane and the holy are part of reality, to be accepted into our life. Without reservation I can recognise the universal truth that our head alone cannot tell all the answers. Our hearts can speak to us of a wider reality, offering deeper insight and answers into life's multitudinous mysteries.

I have learned much on this journey of mine – a process which I hope will continue until the moment I die. I was perhaps more wilful than some, and more stubborn than others, but my mistakes became my teachers and my insights released me from the ashes.

Interview

Q *What, do you think, have your experiences done for you? Can you illustrate the different aspects of your growth?*

I suppose I can identify my *strengths* now, my motivations, abilities, talents and drives. Equally, it seems, I can identify my *weaknesses*: the little fears. The conflicts and complexes as well as some frustrations. I can do that now without any undue mortification.

Q *Can you tell me what brought you to this recognition?*

Yes, I can finally understand myself. I can see why certain things happened – and why I behaved the way I did. I can forgive myself now for the legitimate and the illegitimate guilts. It is clearly all cause and effect. I can finally understand others too – and why they behave the way they do. It took much time and soul-searching though.

Q *Would you say that you are in control of your life?*

As far as we humans can be – and as far as I can judge it, I think I'm not doing too badly. But I am certainly not cocksure about it. I feel a certain stabilising strength within – and because of it I feel humble. I can say that at all times now I am fully prepared to take responsibility for what happens to me and what I do and think.

Q *Have you a way of dealing with problems, difficulties?*

Well, they certainly crop up – and can dismay me, but not for any length of time. I see them as challenges – life's challenges. Something to keep me on my toes, perhaps?

Q *What do you think about failure?*

I suppose my optimism, which is fortunately paired with a good dose of common sense, helps me to confront a bad deal and make the best of it. I endeavour to turn failure around into some kind of success – remembering the wise words of an unknown tutor: 'Failure is not falling down – it is staying down.'

Q *Would you say that your life has helped you to grow?*

The process of 'growing up' brought about a healthy assertiveness and the deep realisation of my identity. My authentic self has been established finally, in a long process of marvellous liberation.

Q *What was, for you, the most significant factor in this 'evolution' of yourself?*

'Glimpses of the truth' increasingly gave me insight into the fact that I am part of a totality – a vast universe. I felt myself to be a microcosm within a macrocosm. It also left me with a deep sense of joy – almost awe – and of safety and connectedness. It seems as if, after a long struggle, I found that the answer to a puzzle (the awareness had been hovering in the background tantalisingly unreachable) had dropped into place – and finally closed the gap, opened my eyes – so to speak. I'm afraid it is well nigh impossible for me to describe just how significant the *spiritual journey* of my life has been

– how love and compassion manifested in a multitude of ways. The liberator is finding our spiritual dimension without losing contact with the practical reality – staying firmly on the ground. Dealing with everyday life and people in harmony between the two. In short, you are free and truly liberated when you can release your ego without losing your identity.

Q *You speak a lot about connectedness – about love – would you explain?*

Many of us feel isolated, separated from the flow of life – from mankind – thinking that this powerful flow, this force, lies beyond – outside ourselves. Yet it is pulsating as a vibrant current through all of us – if we only were to acknowledge it! This force seems to say: I am here for you – take it, or leave it! It is up to you! God's love. Love I liken to a lubricant, oiling the wheels of life, so to speak, smoothly making everything function to its purpose. I believe it is totally unconditional, allowing any one of us to accept this in our own time of growth. There is free will – and choice to grow up and recognise our path.

Q *Can you tell me what you achieve with your method of work?*

I can't think of a better way to explain what I do and achieve other than to let my clients speak for themselves. I therefore include some of the letters I received from clients after their treatments – not because they generally say nice things about me. That, naturally, is very satisfying and heart-warming, but simply to answer your questions more fully and authentically.

Letters

Two letters I have received from clients after their treatments.

I

I first heard of Ellen through a German friend of mine named Inge. Inge had suffered greatly during the war when her family home was taken and her family parted. She came to England virtually penniless, found menial work and eventually met and married a widower. Her husband in his early sixties developed Altzeimer's disease and Inge found it almost impossible to accept that the man she loved was changing daily before her eyes into a stranger she could no longer relate to. Gradually, through her pain, my friend found a spiritual dimension to her life. Our local vicar introduced her to Ellen who through prayer, counselling, deep relaxation and visualization helped Inge to find the inner peace for which she had searched for years. I remember Inge telling me how in a deeply relaxed state Ellen had helped her to visualize being reunited with her husband; as he ran towards her with his arms outstretched their spirits merged. Inge died not many months later, suddenly and peacefully in her sleep. One of the books which helped her resolve difficulties and conflicts from her past was *A Course in Miracles*. With Ellen's help Inge began to live with joy in the present free from all the excess baggage of past hurts. She reached out to others with a new-found love and understanding, and a sense of humour which enriched our lives.

It was at Inge's funeral that I first met Ellen and I was immediately drawn by her vibrant, compassionate, understanding personality. Some weeks later I felt moved by curiosity to find out why I still experienced sadness over my Father's death forty-five years after the event. He had died suddenly when I was seven. Slightly apprehensive, I arrived at Ellen's home for my first consultation. She welcomed me with open arms and that wonderful smile of hers. I felt able to talk, ask questions and to learn about my current attitudes and inner conflicts. With Ellen's skill and knowledge I began to realize the reason for many things happening in my life and why patterns of confrontation occurred and recurred. This realization brought with it the tremendous relief which only knowledge and truth can bring.

Through Ellen's deep relaxation technique and sympathetic visualization I was able to meet my Father in my mind's eye and gradually begin to confront the repressed pain of forty-five years. It was difficult to bear even after all those years but gradually through the copious reading of books recommended by Ellen (each one seeming just right for the next step) and with further counselling and therapy from Ellen I began to be able to face more honestly the good and bad sides of myself and my life. I began my journey of Realization. I discovered I had the power to choose which way my life went. I discovered that self pity, guilt and blaming others are totally negative emotions which hinder the maturing process; also that fear and the past could be released. Most importantly I understood that love and forgiveness of oneself and others are the most powerful gifts for healing available to us.

Further knowledge and personal development came during a course Ellen ran to train Attitudinal Therapists. Five of us learned to lower protective barriers and release more of the truth of our inner selves. This course illustrated what could be achieved through perceptive listening and sharing, led in an intuitive, non-judgemental and caring way by Ellen. She imparted knowledge which she had taken years to acquire herself in the most generous and loving way, treasuring the uniqueness of each individual. This helped each of us to develop our own potentials, accepting our own frailties without being fearful.

I shall always be grateful to Ellen for the love and knowledge she has given so generously.

S.

II

Arriving in my mid-forties with two decent late teenage children, a loving supporting wife, a nice home and an excellent job, it was a shock to feel that life as an unavoidable experience was going downhill. What could be the reason?

On my own the answer seemed unattainable and my dear wife had been suggesting psychiatric assistance which I had resisted. Why, when I was a success in so many things, particularly as a well paid, highly productive workaholic representative working for a market leader in financial services, did I feel a sense of dissatisfaction?

The trail that led to the Von Einem Foundation was convoluted but fortuitous and the results beyond my hopes and expectations.

It had always been my understanding that to succeed in business one needed to drive oneself hard, apply pressure to all concerned and strain for results. However, after a few sessions of 'deep relaxation and attitudinal therapy' here was I relaxed, accepting, calm and peaceful and more of my requests than ever were achieving the desired results.

Manager, colleagues and secretaries noticed a distinct change of approach in mood and general attitude. The family tensions lessened and the whole quality of life improved dramatically.

Twelve months later, I await promotion and occasional lapses are followed by self-adjustment with support, if necessary, from Ellen.

I would recommend attitudinal therapy to all who are stressed, bewildered by success or failure or whose relationships at home and work are stretched to near breaking point – besides those who, like me, were a danger on the roads.

D.